Memories

of a

Lewis Mountain Man

by

John W. Stoneberger

Potomac Appalachian
Trail Club

1993

Copyright © 1993

The Estate of John W. Stoneberger

Edited by Michael E. Monbeck

Published by the
POTOMAC APPALACHIAN TRAIL CLUB, INC.
118 Park Street, S.E.
Vienna, Virginia 22180

Covers: This is the home and some of the 65 acres that W.B. Stoneberger left his family and where John Stoneberger grew up. It is located near where Humes Run begins, just south of Peterfish Gap, in the southern part of Massanutten Mountain (visible here in the background). This photo was taken in the early 1960s. The photograph on the back cover shows the author with his dog Ruffles during a camping trip in the Shendandoah Mountains.

John W. Stoneberger

c. 1952

EDITOR'S PREFACE

The stories and reminiscences of John W. Stoneberger which have been collected in this book were originally written for the *Mountain Laurel*; this informal periodical is produced by Laurel Publications in Wytheville, Virginia, and is devoted to chronicling the life and lore of the Blue Ridge Mountains. In preparing John's writings for publication, I have wielded the editor's pencil as lightly as possible, with my chief function being to eliminate the inevitable repetitions and redundancies that creep into such occasional pieces, while at the same time retaining the original character of his unique and colorful writing style, including his vocabulary, word usage, sentence structure, and so forth. My goal was to let the reader hear John's voice, that is, his way of telling a story, his way of making the life on Lewis Mountain as real as it still was in his mind's eye.

In arranging the pieces, I decided upon the following plan: in the first piece, John briefly introduces himself and sets the stage for his stories; then follows a history of the Roche family on Lewis Mountain, including specifically his maternal grandparents; this is followed by a series of reminiscences of his family, including a short portrait of his mother, a longer one of his father and pieces on three originals, his cousins Alice Lam (the Ridgerunner) and Gerald Allen Lam (the Mountain Storyteller) and his Uncle Mike Roach. After these family-related pieces are 11 stories of the rich life of Lewis Mountain and the Shenandoah Valley. The final piece, though involving a somewhat less than favorable picture of a relative, was one John wanted to tell not only because it provided some balance to his, at times, too rosy picture of his family, but also because it expressed his view (one shared by many mountain people) that it was probably not a very good idea to venture too far "Beyond the Blue Mountains." (Besides, it's a good story.)

In fact, John once wrote of his reason for wanting, in his own way, to document the life of the mountain people as he remembered it; it was to set the record straight. He said, "The mountain people, who left their homes in the Blue Ridge Mountains to make way for the Shenandoah National Park and the Skyline Drive, were not the uneducated dregs of society as some historians have made them out to be. They were God-fearing, hard-working, neighborly people rich in their own heritage; they and their ancestors have proved to be a vital part of the communities that have received them."

I only met John Stoneberger once. Jean Golightly, the PATC's Publications Committee Chairperson, and I were just beginning the preparation of this volume and we arranged to meet with John in order to clarify a few facts that were ambiguous in the manuscript. We also wanted to review the photographs he had in order to match them up with the stories and make a final selection. Fortunately, John had seen a first rough edit and seemed reassured that the tone of his writing and the message he wanted to convey were being respected. Unfortunately, he was far more ill than we had known and, consequently, it was impossible for the book to be published quickly enough for him to see it. Eight days after our visit, on March 17, 1993, John died at his home in Front Royal.

Although John briefly touches on his origins in "A Great Heritage," here are a few facts about his adult life to give us a better sense of the real human being who is telling these stories. After high school at Elkton, John spent a six-month hitch with the CCC (Civilian Conservation Corps) clearing trails, setting shrubbery and trees, and working around the springs. Later, he worked in a quarry and learned to operate heavy construction equipment. In 1945, he began his long career with American Viscose Corporation (now Avtex) and became a first-class compression room operator in the power plant. During employee lay-off periods at Viscose, he would operate heavy equipment for Perry Engineering in Winchester. He retired in 1989. He and his first wife had four children, 13 grandchildren and one great-grandchild. One granddaughter, Allison Nesbitt, was the 1987 Miss Warren County Fair.

In addition to writing down his memories of life on Lewis Mountain, John also loved singing gospel music, reading, and gardening; he traveled regularly to Lewis Mountain to take care of the small family cemetery which contains the graves of seven family members and friends. In addition to his own stories, he once said he would like to see a book written on Front Royal where "we are blessed with two mountains, two rivers, good industry, shopping, highways, and the most beautiful section of the world."

To enhance the presentation of John's stories, we have included a number of family pictures, as well as a few from the same period and area provided by the National Park Service; there is a simple map to orient the reader to the Lewis Mountain area and a family tree to aid the reader in keeping track of the basic family relationships. Finally, to add a personal touch to this very personal document, we have reproduced a two-page sample of John's handwriting.

— Michael E. Monbeck
Fairfax, Virginia
August 30, 1993

TABLE OF CONTENTS

Introduction:

    A Great Heritage.. 1

Grandparents:

    The Lewis Mountain Widow 4

Parents:

    A June Mother 10

    My Dad... 14

Cousins:

    Alice the Ridgerunner................................ 20

    The Lewis Mountain Story Teller.............. 25

Uncle:

    A Tribute to Mike Roach 31

Stories:

    My First Funeral 35

    The Lewis Mountain School...................... 39

    Butchering Day 44

    A Heritage of Music................................... 51

The Lewis Mountain Feast......................... 53

Mountain Moonshine Whiskey 59

That Mule and Me..................................... 62

The Treasure Hunt 66

The Teamster and the Bees 69

Queenie the Mule 74

Beyond the Blue Mountains 77

LIST OF ILLUSTRATIONS

John W. Stoneberger	iii
Bear Fence Mountain	x
Map of the Lewis Moutain Area	xi
John Stoneberger's Handwriting	xii
John and Bill Stoneberger With Bootsie Lam	3
John Scott Roche	8
Cora Virginia Roche	9
Elizabeth Bernice Roche	13
William B. Stoneberger and Friends	15
Alice, the Ridgerunner, Lam	21
Gerald Allen Lam as a Child	24
Gerald Allen Lam, the Lewis Mountain Storyteller	27
Mike Roach	33
The Lewis Mountain School/Pocosin Episcopal #2 Mission	38
Deaconess Carrie G. Makely and the Class of 1915-1916	40
Icie M. Roach and Her Husband	43
Mountain Boy and a Hog	46
Legendary Banjo Player Bela Lam	52
Peeling Bark	54
The Rev. Frank Persons	58
A Mule in Harness	65
A Bark Wagon	70
A Team of Horses	72
A Family Tree	80

Bear Fence Mountain

Author's Note on Locating the Lewis Mountain Home of His Grandparents: If you ever travel the Skyline Drive in the Shenandoah National Park, you pass very near the site of the Roche farm, later the old Lewis Mountain School and the Roche Episcopal Mission. It is a few miles south of Big Meadows, at the point where you pass the "Bear Fence," a large outcrop of rocks, 50 or more feet high, above the trees, and about a half mile long on the crest of the mountain.

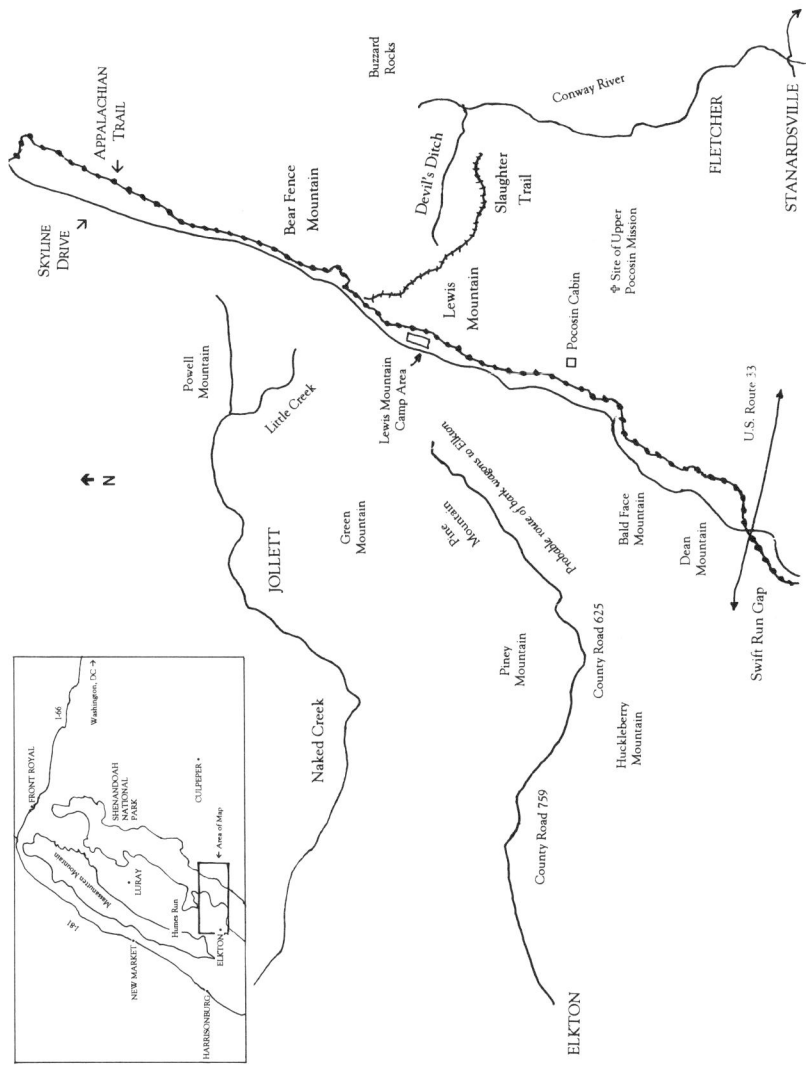

xi

The spring water seemed to tast sweeter and better than any place on earth and the old wood heater didn't feel too bad on a cold nite in a comftable chair as I read "The Call of The Wild" By Jack London.

To watch the cows groze the hills and meadows, watch the chickens under the apple trees, to see the new born Pigs fallow their Mother in spring and watch the fruit trees Blossom, as the bee's made honey and birds built their nest was part of Country life.

To sit under the huge wild cherry tree over our spring on a plesant Summer day and scrape the skin off of new potatoes, about the size of small eggs or marbles, knowing that Mama would be soon preparing dinner and those potatoes would come out of that cast iron skillet, a golden brown where they had been fried in butter, and would be served with new ~~peas~~ peas and June apples and home made cottage cheese....

What else could a country boy ask for? Unless it would be to go into the thick pines to search for those tall slim cedars fishing poles.

A Great Heritage

I like to think of myself as a genuine mountaineer. I was born on Lewis Mountain, located in the central part of what is now Shenandoah National Park, on July 17, 1924, and grew up in the Valley. So I refer to myself as a hillbilly.

The mountain got its name from John Lewis, an English surveyor who, with George Washington, first mapped the area. Lewis received a 244-acre parcel on the mountain through a grant from the English king. His son, Thomas, acquired a number of adjoining parcels until he had about 1,000 acres. He then sold it to a family named Slaughter who held it for some five generations. Sometime in the late 1800s, it was acquired for 50 cents an acre by John Scott Roche and his wife, Cora Virginia Keckley Roche. These were my mother's parents.

Around 1914, W.B. Stoneberger, my father, built a steam-powered sawmill on Lewis Mountain. He had strong, good-natured workers for $1.00 per day and a good steam engine, the best of timber, and good teams. The long trip to market and the low price of lumber soon forced him to return to work as a miner with the Dravo Construction Company at various sites.

While operating the sawmill, however, he had noticed Elizabeth, the 14-year-old daughter of the Roches (whose name was now spelled Roach). And he did not forget her when he reluctantly left the area. When he returned in 1920, he sought out Elizabeth and found that she had grown into a five foot six inch beauty with wavy raven hair. She had also finished her education (including training as a nurse in Hagerstown, Maryland). After they were married, my parents bought a 65-acre, one-horse farm in a secluded area of Rockingham County and built a small five-room house there. When he lost his life in 1924 in a mining accident, my father left a two-year-old son, William B., Jr., and Elizabeth pregnant with me. She returned to her parents' home on Lewis Mountain where I was born about a month later.

And it was here in this heavenly backwoods place that my brother and I grew up, roaming the beautiful hills and meadows on our horse and pony. We never found the gold and treasure we searched for, but were just as happy with what we did find: fresh fruit, lots of berries and nuts, wild game, and abundant fish.

During the years of the Great Depression, we learned to work and make a wonderful living off the land. We enjoyed a comfortable home, plenty to eat, and never noticed that there was very little money. Some of my fondest memories are of the vacations spent with Grandma Roach on Lewis Mountain.

I feel full of gratitude for the rich mountain heritage with which I have been blessed. That is why most of the writing I have done centers around this Lewis Mountain home where life was joyful, love was real, food was good, and rest was peaceful.

As I grew older and after I had retired, I noticed that the love of nature was still in me and so I took a liking to backpacking and to hiking the mountain trails. On one of my trips with my dog Ruffles (half elkhound and half shepherd), we had set up camp for the night at Kennedy Peak on Massanutten Mountain. Just as we sat down to relax, a family of hikers came along the trail. The distinguished looking father said to his family, "Look here, look here. There is a man with everything – he even has his wolf with him!" I was delighted with his remark. Although Ruffles is as gentle as a lamb, she does look exactly like a small wolf.

John W. Stoneberger -- 3

John Stoneberger (left), his brother Bill (center), and their cousin, Montella "Bootsie" Lam.

The Lewis Mountain Widow

I once read the standard version of the Bible through, and in the 58th chapter of Isaiah, I found these words: "In the day that you will feed the hungry, clothe the naked and shelter the needy, then get down on your knees and say, 'Where is this Lord God that made heaven and earth?' Then will I answer and say, 'Here I am!'"

My grandmother, Cora Virginia Roche, born January 19, 1868, and died September 16, 1936, came as close to living the 58th chapter of Isaiah as any one I ever knew. She was the real backbone of our spiritual heritage. She was born a Keckley and married a Reynolds, a man of fine character and reasonable wealth, who died and left her with three children. In 1892, she formed a union with John Scott Roche who was in a similar situation: his wife had died and left him with seven children.

Grannie moved from Lost River, West Virginia, to Lewis Mountain near Elkton, Virginia, where they bought 1,000 acres, with a large, well-built home made from hand-hewn logs and with a large fireplace in both the living room and extended kitchen. It was here that they finished raising their combined families, plus seven more children of their own; my mother, Elizabeth, was one of these.

Every mountain seems to bear a lovable character: Moses got his calling on Mt. Horeb, the Rev. Bob Childress on Buffalo, and Cora Roche on Lewis. There were more signs of God reigning in that mountain age than in our present times of modern technology. People gave with love, even if it was a piece of cornbread or a baked sweet potato.

They knew that giving was the life blood of mountain life; without generosity life would have been almost impossible. It was by the giving of labor, milk, food, seed, and sharing of animals, tools, and guns that they were able to survive. They knew the joy of sacrifice without a thought of reward. It seemed the rugged mountain life brought out the noblest qualities in people.

This couple knew that in the Highlands of Scotland many a man had worked a lifetime, died and left a will of his earthly possessions which consisted of two oxen, a plow, bed, table, four chairs and four bowls. In Scotland, much of the crops went to the king and his men, with little being left for the tenant. The Blue Ridge Mountains of Virginia offered high hopes of prosperity for these people with such rich natural resources as fertile soil, good timber, abundant water, and lots of bluegrass grazing land and meadows. Fruit (apples, peaches, cherries) and chestnuts were plentiful, along with wild game and trout. It was like the Garden of Eden to Cora and John Scott Roche. Grannie and Grandpa had brought their education with them into the mountains, but now their main concern was how to bring education to their children.

Grandpa was a man of good judgment in business and management, with 30 men peeling bark in the spring of the year for the tannery in Elkton (each trip was 30 miles round-trip and took two days) and keeping a four-mule team with harness and wagon in shape for other work year around. With looking after cattle (he had some 150 head), fencing, and patch farming, he was a busy man.

Grannie was just as busy, plus she saw the great lack of knowledge in the mountains for both church and school. She was well acquainted with the Great Mother Church of England (the Anglican Church) and here she sent for help.

The Reverend Frank Persons, a very congenial young minister, was sent to live in the Roche home and to conduct all religious services for the community. A chapel was built onto the house and used until the number of people required a larger meeting house. Later, after Grandpa died (April 10, 1917), she gave 10 acres of land with timber, along with the use of her sawmill, to build the new St.

Andrews Roche Mountain Mission. There were eight or more Episcopal missions in the area from Simmons Gap to Big Meadows as well as several mission homes staffed with registered nurses. These homes were used like hospitals; much food and labor came from the local mountaineers to help maintain these stations of mercy. The missions were under the supervision of Archdeacon Frederick W. Neve. The church also had a high school at Yancy (or Lynwood), plus the large Blue Ridge Industrial School at Dyke.

In the early days of Grannie's life on Lewis Mountain, before the mission was established, she had her family organized so that each sister had a younger child to care for. A book could be written on how a sister learned to mother a younger brother or sister and how the love that developed lasted a lifetime. The real purpose of it was so Grannie could set her home in order, and saddle a horse in the morning to ride through the mountains to help a mother give birth, wait on the sick, or shroud the dead. She could do the work of a midwife, maid, cook, nurse, and minister. They say, "To be loved, needed, and wanted is the greatest calling on earth." Grannie had all these things and used them well.

Grandpa was known as the mountain prophet, but one day he came under conviction and found his faith and called for the Bishop of the church to come hear his confession, pray with him, and baptize him. Carrie Mackley, an Episcopal teacher, lived in his home in 1916 and noted the event in her diary (of which I have a copy).

Grandpa, who was older than Grannie, left her a widow in 1917. She continued to live on Lewis Mountain until her land became part of the Shenandoah National Park in 1934.

I read a lot where writers mention poor widows. Grannie was twice a widow: 1890-1892 and from 1917 until her death in 1936. One thing I would love to declare is that she never was poor! She believed her Bible and knew riches and honor could walk hand in hand with loving and giving.

A cousin told me a story about when the men came with the big truck to move her from Lewis Mountain to Rhodesville, Virginia. As the fellows struggled with a heavy camel-back trunk, the bottom fell out and they discovered it was filled with jars of money! At this time, she had been a widow for 17 years.

By 1934, most people had moved out of the mountains because

of the formation of the Shenandoah National Park and because high-paying jobs in coal mining, steel making and other industries had called to them. One of the last to go was a young family who lived near Grannie; they owned no home, had little money, and had no place to go. Grannie bought them a home with 20 acres of land.

This fine family later repaid every penny of her gift, plus many kind deeds, favors, and presents. I like to think of the widow in the Bible who was blessed for making the Prophet Elijah a cake with the last bit of her oil and meal.

Grannie gave both room and board to ministers and teachers for years. She helped raise dozens of children and was host to large numbers on holidays and weekends. At funerals, church picnics, and mutton feasts, she fed hundreds. What I liked about her is that she gave from the top of her barrel.

Yes, Prophet, we do believe those who will feed the hungry, clothe the naked and shelter the needy will be blessed by God. This is pure religion, the kind that true mountaineers love.

(1990)

Author's Note: I want to express here the deep gratitude I feel for Archdeacon Frederick W. Neve, the Rev. Frank Persons, and Deaconess Carrie G. Makely, along with the Episcopal Church, who aided, cared for the sick, and met the spiritual needs of the Lewis Mountain people of Greene County, Virginia, in the early 1900s.

John Scott Roche (1849-1917)

John W. Stoneberger --- 9

Cora Virginia Roche (1868-1936) **with John W. Stoneberger and William, his older brother**

A June Mother

          I think June is the most wonderful month in the year. The blue skies are the bluest, the white clouds are the whitest, the grass is the greenest, flowers smell the sweetest, and roses are the dewiest.

    My mother was the daughter of John Scott and Cora Virginia Roche of Lewis Mountain, near Elkton, Virginia. Her maiden name was Elizabeth Bernice Roche and she was born here on June 24, 1899. She was heaven's great gift to me. I was born without knowledge and had to learn; you could have put a cabbage leaf over my eyes and told me the sky was falling and I probably would have believed it. But one thing I always seemed to know, my mother's love was real, and she would never leave me or forsake me.

    In August 1978, she went to the hospital; her stay lasted 19 days. I suffered with her every day, prayed, and mustered all the faith I could for her recovery. I often wondered if my grief would also kill me if she died. On September 16, 1978, at 4:30 in the morning, I received the call telling me that she had died. As I knelt beside my bed and prayed to thank God for Mama's well needed rest, a heavenly peace came over me, one of the most pleasant and shocking surprises I ever had! It wasn't her death that was so terrible, but her sickness and suffering that had been causing me such misery and discomfort.

    What a blessed man I am to have had such a precious mother. She cared for me in life, sheltered me, fed me, nursed me in sickness, taught me the way of salvation, and, before she left this world, I had everything a man would want. I knew how to be set free from sin, to walk righteously before God, to face the future with a good conscience and hope of eternal life.

On Mother's Day, I say, "Thank God of Heaven for the gift of a beautiful, loving, June Mother."

(1990)

The Old Cemetery

    I like to go to the cemetery
    And give my mind a rest.
    I think of life as it unrolled
    And how that I was blessed.
        Mama she was precious
        And life was full of joy,
        My life was full and happy
        When I was a little boy.
    The first day that I went to school,
    A heavy dew had fell, and
    The drone of those busy bees
    On those scented flowers was swell.
        We lived out in the country
        Beside those springs and stream.
        The flowers were so pretty
        And the bees were not too mean.
    As I learned what life was all about,
    Some great surprises came that
    Life has many pleasures, sorrows, hurts and pain.
    And with these things a faith must go
        To help you on your way,
        To bring both love and forgiveness,
        To heal the hurts and pain
        That we can enjoy the sunshine and rain.
    For the many errors we make in life,
    I am glad there is a way
    To repent and find forgiveness

That will brighten up our day.
    As I sit here on the stone,
    I am glad that I can say,
    As I look into the future,
    I am glad I found the way.
A better place is waiting
For those who have the grace
To muster up their courage
And run a strenuous race.
    Here at your tombstone, Mama,
    I would like to take the time
    To tell you that I love you
    and everything is fine.
Through many trials and errors,
I have found that blessed grace
And I know that it will take me
To that blessed resting place.
    I thought it would be easy,
    When I knelt there at your knee,
    But I found I had to struggle
    To really meet my needs.
I found God's grace sufficient,
As you told me it would be,
And my bright hope of heaven
Is as real as it can be.
    So, once again, dear Mama,
    I would like to take this time
    To tell you that I love you
    And everything is fine.

Elizabeth Bernice Roche (c.1919)

My Dad

My father, William B. Stoneberger was born in Elkton, Virginia, on March 16, 1892. His parents, who had eight children, were Hiram and Lola Stoneberger.

Once Hiram went riding and had stuck a small rifle into his boot with the barrel pointing up and the stock down. When the gun accidentally discharged, he was fatally wounded. Lola died just a few years later, thus orphaning the eight children. Since there were no Stoneberger relatives to help and there was no welfare department in Rockingham County in the early 1900s (Harrisonburg didn't get a hospital until 1912!), the only choice the children had was to bond together and make out the best they could. The eldest girl became the mother and the older boys looked for ways to earn a bit of money to help the family to survive.

The old Stoneberger home was on a high plateau near Greenwood. The 360-degree view from the house included the Blue Ridge Mountains in front and the Massanutten in the back. In summer, the scene was spectacular, although in winter a bone-chillingly cold northwest wind would sweep across the ridge.

The old house had rocks for a foundation and brick for the chimney. The sides consisted of vertical boards with strips nailed over the cracks. The steep roof was of wooden shingles and had some narrow windows. There were four rooms and a loft. The doors were hand-made. It appeared to have been built with good lumber. Over the years, much rain, sleet, hail, and snow had bleached the unpainted wood and turned it a deep gray. Nevertheless, the old place still looked strong and durable.

There were about two acres of land with different kinds of fruit trees, including lots of cherry. There was a large garden in front of the house and a deep, never-failing, hand-dug well for water. Near

My father, William B. Stoneberger, is in the center of this studio gag picture, with some friends who worked with him in the mines, including (at lower left) Uncle Jerry Roche, Mama's oldest brother.

the well in the garden was a small structure built over a cellar in the ground. Potatoes, onions, home-canned food, and meat, if they had any, were stored in this cellar to keep them from both spoiling and freezing. Nearby were several big walnut trees. My Uncle Mike Roach, a man of good judgment, told me, "The area of your Dad's old place was the poorest looking country I ever saw."

In spite of everything that was against them, the children believed in themselves and in their ability to make a life for themselves. They learned at an early age that it was "Root, little pig, or lose your tater."

It seemed that the loss of both parents drew them closer together. Good clothes and heat were precious; trying to find ways to help was a joy. They found that by working, praying, and sticking together, they could make it.

By having the old estate garden and well, these orphaned children managed to feed and clothe themselves, *and* receive an education at the Old Humes Run School.

When my brother Bill and I were boys, we found one of our Dad's old rabbit box-traps. It was made from cedar lumber and he had carved his initials into the well-worn wood. We thought: with this old box, Dad must have put many a delicious rabbit on the table and all when he was a boy about our age!

The older boys would ride freight trains to apple pickings to make money. When Dad was only three or four years old, he heard them talking and said, "When I grow up to be a man, I want to bum a freight train." Someone heard him and said, "So, you want to be a bum. Well, we'll just start calling you *bum* right now." He was known by that nickname from then on. All my life, women have hugged my neck and men shaken my hand, smiled, and said, "It's so nice to meet Bum's boy."

The orphaned children had no parents to teach them religious ways, but they did have chapel in school, and had good in their hearts, and knew right from wrong.

After Uncle Dick was a man, he saw a fellow take a woman into the old Stoneberger house when there was no one at home. This angered him and, as he walked toward the house, he pulled a paling off of the yard fence. He quietly walked into the bedroom and hallowed "Get out of here!" and hit the man over the rump! This fellow ran the hundred yards out the lane to the main road, pulling up his pants in front with one hand with his white shirttail flying in the breeze. You could still see the red stripe on his rump when he turned the corner. No one remembers him ever coming back.

My Dad once cut himself in the calf with a sharp wood ax and came home bleeding terribly. He said, "Josie, sew my leg up." She knew he would bleed to death before he could ride a horse three miles to town to see a doctor and so she got a needle and thread and said, "I can't do it, but you can!" When he had put the last stitch in, he fell back on the bed and almost passed out! I asked Mama about the story and she said, "Yes, it is true, the stitches were still in his leg when we got married – he had sewed it up with black thread!"

In November and February, they cut land cress from the wheat fields. In early spring, they searched for water cress, polk greens, dandelion, plantain, and mushrooms. They picked wild strawberries, blackberries, raspberries, chinquapins, walnuts, hazelnuts, and hickory nuts. Wild game, mostly rabbits and squirrels (but once in a while raccoon, muskrat, groundhog, and quail), were enjoyed; they also ate trout and turtle fish. Everything was cherished and relished. I think Stoneberger cooks are the best on earth; among their best are jams and jellies, especially quince.

Along the Shenandoah River by the Henry Carrier farm is an old fishing place called the Sand Bank. The river here flows against a huge rock cliff about 85 feet high and bends left. Melvin McCoy said, "I have saw the Stoneberger boys dive off of that rock into the deep hole of water many a time." It would almost take my breath away to think about a dive like that! They were venturous young men and, although each only had a fourth- or fifth-grade education, four of them became construction foremen. My Dad worked for Dravo, a company in Pittsburgh. He drilled tunnels through many mountains and sank shafts deep into the earth. Once when he returned home from a job where he had made big money, he bought a huge steam engine and built a sawmill on Lewis Mountain.

On June 15, 1924, in Detroit, Michigan, where Dravo was sinking a salt mine shaft, the shaft inspector went down first for his inspection and didn't come back! Next, Mr. Burn, the foreman, went down and he didn't come back! Mr. Gott, the superintendent, put the big bucket on the cable and took two men, including my Dad, down the shaft with him. Neither Mr. Gott nor my Dad returned. The other man was brought up in the bucket and he was unconscious! Four miners had died because chlorine gas was coming out of a crack in the wall like blue smoke. Without warning, it had knocked each man unconscious and then, falling into three feet of water, was drowned.

As a small boy, my Dad had a determination to go somewhere in life even if he had to bum a freight train to get there. He climbed some of the tallest rocks in the Shenandoah Valley and dived into one of the deepest holes of water in the Shenandoah River. With a fourth-grade education, he worked as foreman for the world's largest construction company and made top money. He bought his own steam engine and sawmill and then moved it some 20 miles to Lewis Mountain. When he got to the mountain area, as many as 100 people would come up on foot or horse each day to watch the machine puff and work. It was at this time that he met and married a beautiful girl, Elizabeth B. Roach. They bought 65 acres near his old home and built a new five-room house. Soon, however, as he told his friend, Monroe Douel, "I need to go back to the construction job one more time for some big money, then I want to settle down at home and raise a family." Unfortunately, it was on this job that he lost his life. He is buried at the old St. Peter's Church Cemetery at Humes Run. A beautiful marble tombstone marks his grave. On top of the stone is carved an open Bible and the inscription "God moves in a mysterious way."

Although my Dad died a month before I was born, his life has been an inspiration to me. He was strong and virtuous and had the courage to pursue his dream. He owned a Henderson motorcycle and a horse, both of which he loved to race.

He only lived 32 years, but his pleasure in life and his accomplishments were good. I grew up in the home he left us and part of my daily prayer is still "Thank you, Lord, for all my Dad gave me."

Inspiration, courage, faith, ambition, and moderation are some of the many things he left me, plus the old home-place where we made our living during the Great Depression years. Here we enjoyed the fresh mint- and flower-scented air in summer; whippoorwills sat on the porch railings and called at night. We also enjoyed many a restful night as rain hammered the tin roof in a restful rhythm to sleep by.

The spring water seemed to taste sweeter and better than any place on earth and the old wood heater didn't feel too bad on a cold night in a comfortable chair as I read *The Call of the Wild* by Jack London. To watch the cows graze the hills and meadows, to watch the chickens under the apple trees, to see the newborn pigs follow their mother in spring, and to watch the fruit trees blossom as the bees made honey and the birds built their nests were all part of country life.

Country life was also sitting under the huge wild cherry tree over our spring on a pleasant summer day and scraping the skin off of new potatoes, about the size of small eggs or marbles. It was knowing that Mama would soon be preparing dinner and those potatoes would come out of that cast-iron skillet a golden brown where they had been fried in butter and would be served with new peas and June apples and home-made cottage cheese. What else could a country boy ask for, unless it would be to go into the thick pines to search for those tall slim cedar fishing poles?

On Father's Day, we offer a special prayer to the Lord and say thank you for Dad.

Author's Note: One day, my Dad lay down on the bed and put his head in the bend of his arm. Mama said, "Bumbsie, are you all right? It's not like you to lay down in daytime."

He answered, "Yes, I'm all right. I'm preparing myself for a better world."

This is the main purpose in my life: to be a loving, kind-hearted mountaineer, to do all the good I can in this world, and prepare myself for a better place.

Alice the Ridgerunner

Most everything I have written for publication and for republication in *Memories of a Lewis Mountain Man* relate to my life and that of my forebears in the Blue Ridge Mountains, but these pieces wouldn't be complete unless I mentioned Alice the Ridgerunner. She is a chip off of the old block, namely Cora V. Roche, "The Lewis Mountain Widow," our grandmother. As I tell the truth about the chip, it will sound more like fiction than truth.

When Alice was a little girl, she was a typical tomboy. Her folks enjoyed visiting Grannie Roche who had a little pet sow with four or five pigs. She was friendly and loving. She lived around the grassy yard, walked through the spring branch water, and appeared as clean as a pin.

Alice was four years old and she had learned to ride the sow as it went around the yard or in the meadow where it searched for food. It seemed that the sow and pigs enjoyed the play as much as she did. When lunch time came for the pigs one day, their mother lay down on the clean grass and stretched herself out so the pigs could nurse. Alice saw that it was the right time to make the other children laugh, so she pretended she was a pig and would eat with them. This caused much laughter and made Alice's day.

At the South River picnic ground on the Skyline Drive, during a Roche family reunion some 60 years later, someone told the story of Alice and the pigs and asked Alice if the story was true! Alice replied, "Yes, it's true and it was good, too!" This brought about the most joyful laugh of the day. Alice was still at it!

In the fall of last year [1989], Alice was very sick for a while. When I went to see her, she was some better. She went on to say how nice and loving the neighbors, the minister, church members, and kinfolk had been to bring her gifts of special food and flowers, and especially their prayers for her. Then came her line, "Why, being sick wouldn't be bad at all, if you just didn't have to feel so bad." This is real mountain humor.

Later, she found out that she needed a gall stone operation. She wrote and told me about someone breaking into a home in the area and taking a lot of valuables while the people worked the night shift. She went on to say she didn't mind going to the hospital for the

Alice, the Ridgerunner, Lam (1944)

operation, but she didn't like to leave her home with no one there. Then came another Alice line: "Suppose someone broke in my home while I was in the hospital and got in my rag pile. Why, they could get on my sewing machine and make a half dozen quilts and I wouldn't be able to tell they had been there and got anything. Wouldn't that be terrible?" (Alice loves to sew and makes quilts by the hundreds. Her supplies can take up a big part of a room and this is what she calls her rag pile.)

At one time she cared for seven sick, aged invalids and handicapped people. She washed their clothes, carried them food, cut their hair, prayed with them, and did whatever she could to help them. She would never take any money for her service.

Once an extra-large man who ran a service station/grocery store with a carry-out beer business needed her help as a live-in nurse. He told her that all went well until he would have to go to the hospital and then someone always broke in his business at night. When it came time for him to be readmitted, he gave her a large pistol and told her what to expect.

As Alice told the story, she heard someone rattling the storm door one night. In the dark, she quietly slipped the latch off the lock of the main door so the intruder wouldn't break the door as had been done several times before. With the gun in hand, she walked to the other side of the room and stood next to the light switch. When the burglar walked in, she put the light on and, with the pistol pointed at him, asked, "What do you want?"

He answered with an "Oh! My Lord!" and then backed out of the room with his arms stretched straight up in the air. He lay face down on the hood of a car for a minute or so and it appeared that he was praying. Then, he raised up and said, "Thank you, lady, for not shooting me!"

Alice said, "I'm glad I didn't shoot you this time, but I want you to know if you ever try that trick on me again, the undertaker will be stuffing cotton up your backside before the sun goes down."

At church, Alice was once asked to testify and with good delivery she expressed gratitude for the love of God and His marvelous Grace. She also said she was glad she had been born poor because learning how to struggle and do well for yourself and others was a big part of the joy of life.

Someone told a tale on a man who, years ago, would ride a big sorrel mule to Fields Day at Elkton, where he would drink whiskey, set his hat a bit sideways, and really enjoy the day. Once he had come home hungry in between meals and found an iron pot of warm food on the old woodstove. He took a big spoon and began to eat out of the pot. When his wife came in, she said, "You should have put the food in a bowl." He answered, "Go away, Malindie, I have ate the broth, and I am just beginning to get down to the noodles!"

The reason I like Alice is that she is full of humor, love, and goodness, as well as law and order. She knows that the noodles of life are at the bottom of the pot. She is so much like Grannie Roche in sheltering the needy, feeding the hungry, and clothing the naked. To her, the joy of life is in helping others.

Alice gave me the first mountain laurel I ever saw and has given me stories and pictures to help me in writing mountain history. I once ate at her house and she had a big mess of cured pig's feet, home-made sauerkraut, and cherry cobbler pie; in short, all good eating and all favorites of mine.

Alice rode the hog and ran the ridges for chestnuts, apples, cherries, and berries. She also could catch the trout, trap the rabbit, snitch the apples, dry the beans, and bake the best coconut cake for family reunions. She learned to do special sewing as a child; she could harness a horse or mule and plow the garden, trim the hedge, and prune a tree.

When she was young, Alice could run the neck of a guitar and pick out "Don't Let Your Deal Go Down" that was pleasing to hear. By the way, she is related to the famous Lam family, who for four generations made the best string music in the Blue Ridge Mountains. Four of her children are also musicians (Charles on Dobro, Fuzzy on guitar, Debby on piano, and Dick on banjo).

So, you can see that we all love Alice the Ridgerunner because she is the real "noodles" of life on Lewis Mountain. Anyone who would try to excel Alice in tricks, humor, love, and goodness, kindness and mercy, law and order, and telling it like it is, I think would find that "she would be a hard cat to shave."

Gerald Allen Lam as a Child (1920s)

The Lewis Mountain Storyteller

John Scott Roach had a daughter named Nellie, who was a very beautiful woman, tall with a pretty head of wavy black hair. She married Virgil Lam and her second child was a strong, handsome boy with hair like his Mom and Dad; his name was Gerald Allen Lam, born May 18, 1915.

The Blue Ridge Mountain children were considered some of the healthiest in the world. They overcame minor ailments easily. Crib death and tuberculosis were the two most dreaded diseases until there was an outbreak of infantile paralysis about 1919. Gerald Allen was a victim of this terrible disease. It left him crippled for life and his once strong body became thin, with very weak wrists and ankle joints enlarged to three times their normal size. He did manage to walk by himself in a very awkward way, swaying to control the weak joints with a wobbly balance.

I believe life is somewhat like a great wrestling match. With determination, faith, will power and suffering, one can find a counter for every hold and any disappointment can be turned into an advantage. So it was with Gerald Allen. He learned to listen carefully and became Lewis Mountain's greatest storyteller.

A day would never get too hot or cold, dark or rainy, that Gerald couldn't make me laugh. A great volume could have been written of his tales and the following are a few of them. I only wish I could tell them half as well as Gerald.

The Junior Lodge of Elkton, Virginia, started a yearly event called Fields Day along the beautiful Shenandoah River where there was plenty of shade and a bluegrass lawn, plus a full program of contests, prizes, pony and mule racing, ball game, carnival, concession stands, etc., all to provide a day of fun, festivity, entertainment and fellowship for a small fee. The event drew the largest crowds of all times in this section of the county, with both the Valley and mountain people attending for miles around.

Aunt Nellie met Mama there for the day. Both of them had brought their small children, one of them being Gerald Allen. After the greeting, joy of meeting, brief news, and so on, Mama invited all to have a hot dog and a cold soft drink. As each child was being served, Gerald began to cry like his heart would break! Quick as a flash, Mama realized that Gerald was used to pure mountain food and didn't know what mustard was. When Gerald got older, he one day said, "Aunt Elizabeth, you are such a good woman. Do you remember when I was a little boy and I thought some bad cat had put yellow mustard on my hot dog? I cried and couldn't eat it, but you got me another one."

Gerald grew up in a large family of hard-working mountain people who had much to do (tending cattle, gardening, picking fruit, patch farming, canning, and many other chores). Gerald was a good child and, being crippled, required no extra attention from anyone, but was expected to look after himself as the others worked.

There came a time when he became so quiet and contented, they thought that someone had better check and see what he was doing. His dad followed the crippled boy to a log building where he had been spending a lot of time. Here they found him playing in the soft dry dirt under a porch that sat on tall posts. He was pretending that he was operating a sawmill. Much work had been spent in preparing the sawmill seat, but the shocking surprise was that he had trained two large rattlesnakes to be harnessed with strings and for him to use them for his horses to drag the logs to the mill. He told me after he was a man about how it hurt him to see his dad kill those snakes, "but now I am as afraid of snakes as you are."

Gerald would need to get a special job when he grew up and so he was sent to Fredricksburg to be trained as a first-class jeweler and watchmaker. The idea was that he could then set up shop in Shenandoah, which he did and where the Norfolk-Western Railroad men gave him a large part of his business. He often entertained his customers with amusing tales and they in turn did the same for him.

Heavyweight prizefighting was a special interest around that time. On fight nights, country stores would fill up with "fans" who came to listen to the round-by-round results on the radio. Once when the subject was being discussed in Gerald's shop, a huge railroad engineer named Jim said, "I once went to New York where the heavyweight boxers were training. They had a big set of scales on a wall with a padded device that could register how many pounds a boxer could deliver in one punch. I observed these very strong fellows deliver punches of 600 and 700 pounds! So then I told them that I was not a boxer, but a railroad man, and asked if I could hit the thing just once. With their consent, I plowed a hard right into it and it showed 1,440 pounds."

Gerald replied, "Man alive, Jim, that's as hard as a horse could kick it!"

Gerald Allen Lam

Another of Gerald's stories goes like this: A neat, little old woman was at her wood pile and had a one-man saw that was too heavy for her. When a bum came by and asked her for a meal, she told him she would be glad to prepare him a good meal, if he would saw up a few blocks of wood for her. He said he was hungry and weak and would have to eat first. So, she prepared his meal, he ate it and then started walking toward the wood pile. She assumed he would saw wood while she cleaned the kitchen. When she looked out the window to see how he was doing, however, she didn't see him. She walked out to the wood pile where she found a note which said, "You *saw* me coming, you gave me the *saw*, but you didn't see me *saw*."

Here's another of Gerald's Lewis Mountain tales: A small young man went to Elkton and committed some small infractions of the law. Officers with a warrant came the 15 miles on horseback to arrest him. The mountain people had much sympathy for the fellow and felt he was a good person who by ignorance had made some slight mistakes. Everyone believed that if he would hide a few times when the officers came looking for him, they would soon get tired of coming and forget all about it. One day, the officers arrived while he was in the living room. With plain furniture, there was not really any place for him to hide. A lady told him to get down on his hands and knees and pretend he was a bench; she threw a spread over him and two of the children sat on him until the officers left.

Another time he was in the kitchen when the officers showed up. The owner of the home was a large, very dignified lady who was wearing a hoop skirt that came down to the floor. When she heard the officers coming, she grabbed the man and put him under her skirt. The officers asked if she had seen him and she replied, "Yes, I saw him. I am sure he is close by somewhere, but I can't see him now." After the officers left, she got very angry, reached under her skirt, and got him by the back of his neck. She raised him to his feet, shook him, and, in a harsh tone, said, "What are you doing under there? Don't ever let me catch you under there again!"

Gerald would talk on the spiritual side of life sometimes and his words were very effective. He once said, "I loved to go to Sunday School in Jollet Hollow and sit with my uncle George Meadows who was an extra large, robust, well-built, 260-pound man with a 20-inch neck, muscular arms and rosy cheeks. As I would sit and look at Uncle George, I would think 'What a contrast! He is built like a big saw log and I am like a thin fence rail.' "

One Sunday he said, "If I could have one wish in life come true, I would like to be as big and strong as Uncle George! Could you believe, before the next Sunday rolled around, Uncle George had a heart attack and died. I was looking at him in his casket wondering how this could be. That was 35 years ago and I am still here."

Another time, Gerald mentioned that his grandmother had once killed a wild bear with an ax. I questioned him for the details of the story and this is what he told me. Her name was Mary Lam and she lived on Lewis Mountain near the stream of Devil's Ditch. She was talented at many things and had once won a wood-chopping contest at a Mutton Festival against an aged man who was the champion. One day she was picking cherries. The baby was in a basket and two small children were nearby in the meadow under a tree. She saw the bear and moved close to her children with her ax. The bear circled the tree eating fallen cherries as though no one was around. She could see that he was going to pass within a few feet of her and in a stealthy way she raised the ax and quickly and forcefully sent the sharp blade into the bear's skull as he tried to pass. You have to admire her love for her children, her willingness to protect them, her courage, and her physical strength. You also have to recognize her good fortune to be putting a good roast of bear on the supper table that night, along with a cherry cobbler pie, with the bonus of a bear skin sleeping bag for the baby.

On March 14, 1912 (three years before Gerald was born), a political war broke out in the court house at Hillsville and was noticed in the news around the world. A fine group of mountaineers named Allen were involved and I had often wondered if the incident had any influence on Gerald Allen Lam's name. I think perhaps it did, because I do know that he was a real mountaineer and, as such, a lover of guns. He had steady nerves, good eyes and was a crack shot with any kind of gun.

On a Sunday morning, soon after he moved his business to Second Street in Shenandoah, Gerald dressed in his finest suit, white shirt, tie, well-polished shoes, beautiful head of well-trimmed and well-groomed hair. In his belt, he then inserted a large .38

caliber Smith & Wesson pistol with walnut-engraved handle grips and a six-inch blue steel barrel. Thus decked out, he buttoned his coat and wobbled over to the big Baptist Church on Third Street.

About half way through the lesson, he unbuttoned his coat and shifted his position so that his beautiful gun would show, all the while seeming to take a deep interest in the lesson. He came home somewhat disappointed, however, because no one noticed his gun.

If the minister or the Sunday School teacher would have asked why he brought his gun to church, I feel sure I could have answered them in this way. "Don't you know our right to worship God is the greatest privilege ever extended to a man and, if I were you, I would have two automatics of the finest caliber."

He had a great sense of humor and was the greatest entertainer. Mountain life was more enjoyable and exciting than most people would think and Gerald Allen Lam was the one who could tell Lewis Mountain stories best of all.

I once asked Gerald if he ever had any great aspirations in life that he had failed to accomplish. He said, "No, but when I die, I want to be buried on the Great Prairie." I suppose he felt he belonged there with the great heroes.

He died on August 3, 1976, and is buried in Prospect Hill Cemetery at Front Royal where I also have a grave site. On the great Resurrection morning, should Gerald rise and attain eternal life, I hope he can be himself with a body like Uncle George's. We can then meet those great prairie heroes and swap tales with them for a long time. Gerald Allen Lam, we miss your stories. H-A-W, H-A-W, H-A-W was the way he laughed.

(1988)

A Tribute to Mike Roach

My uncle and my mother's older brother was Michael B. Roach, who was born on April 4, 1902, in Pocosin Hollow on Lewis Mountain. In 1923, he married Lina E. Taylor (a twin daughter of Sylvanis and Lilly Taylor) at Jollett Hollow Methodist Church. Mike and Lina had five children: Marie, John, Betty, Frances, and Elizabeth.

About the time Mike was 10 or 12 years old, the Saint Andrew's Roach Mountain Mission and School was being established on Lewis Mountain. It was a busy time for everyone and the future looked bright and progressive for the mountain folk. Things were happening that had never before happened on the mountain: hundreds of cattle were grazing, the mule-drawn bark wagon was making two trips a week to Elkton, the Mission and School was open, and a steam-driven sawmill was going to be built.

Mike had grown up on this 1,000-acre "estate" with its more than 100 bark roads and innumerable trails leading off of each road. Our old Episcopal Church papers say, "Mike is such a loving and congenial young man [that he] walks long distances through all kinds of weather almost daily to carry the mail and packages for the Pastor, missionaries and their families." As the load got heavier and he got older, Mike used a horse or mule under saddle or, when needed, a light wagon to do this job. When he was full-grown, Mike stood more than six feet tall, weighed more than 200 pounds, and was extra strong. He had also become quite skillful with tools.

For miles around Mike was considered one of the best at building fences. Not only could he split 200-300 eleven-foot rails a day, he could make a fence that was "horse high, bull strong, and pig tight." He was so strong that he could pick up a 100-pound anvil by the horn and toss it about like a toy.

Our home had a screen door with a spring to pull it closed, but there was no latch. One day a snake crawled into the kitchen and we saw the cat playing with it under a cabinet. Mama disliked this and she spoke to Mike about the incident. He arrived shortly with a handful of tools (a small drill, saw, chisel, screwdrivers, and pocket knife). I watched very closely as he worked with his materials: a piece of oak scrap for the body, a piece of hickory for the latch, a piece of yellow locust for the spring, four wood screws, and a leather string. In a very few minutes, he made a professional looking latch for our door which from then on would latch securely every time it was closed. It never gave a bit of trouble and lasted for years. It was the neatest piece of craftsmanship I had ever seen. From that time on, I always loved tools and wanted to become a craftsman.

Around 1920, my Dad, his brothers, and brother-in-law Mike worked for Dravo Construction Company of Pittsburgh, the largest company of its kind in the world at the time. A lot of the work they did involved drilling mineshafts and driving tunnels deep into the earth or through mountains. One day, Mike was working in a deep shaft mucking around the big bucket when a piece of steel reinforcement fell from the top of the shaft, piercing Mike in the back and coming out in the pelvic area. I think of the awful agony he must have suffered as he was loaded in the hoisting bucket, raised to the surface, and then taken to the hospital. But I also know that he was strong and tough and knew how to pray.

After the terrible accident in the shaft, Mike had trouble with rupture in the lower part of his body and was forced to seek lighter work. He found employment in Fall River, Massachusetts, and that was where he raised his family.

It was a joy to be in Uncle Mike's presence and his mountain humor was the best. For example, when I was young, he came to dinner with my family. My mother, who could make jelly, jam, or preserves of just about any fruit wild or domestic, passed a jar of her latest creation (made from fox grapes) to Uncle Mike and said, "Mike, can you tell me what this is? I know it is not jelly or preserves

Mike Roach as a young man

and seems more like a jam." He carefully put a teaspoon of it on half of a buttered biscuit, slowly ate it, chewed on it a while, and seemed like he was in deep thought. We kids could hardly wait for his answer when he said, "I can tell you exactly what it is – Killum Quick!" We thought that was the funniest thing we had ever heard. And we enjoyed that jam all winter, remembering our favorite uncle and always saying, "Please pass the Killum Quick!"

Once, after he had joined a secret order, he knew that a neighbor lady with a most inquisitive mind would never leave him alone until he answered her questions. Since he was sworn to secrecy, he made up the following story so he would be ready for her.

"The first thing they did was take me to a long, dark tunnel and asked me if I could see the little red light at the end of the tunnel. I said that I could. Then they told me to start crawling on my hands and knees toward the light and I was not to stop or let anything distract me until I got there. In obedience to this command, I started crawling. Soon, on my left, I saw a beautiful blond young lady in her night clothes on a comfortable bed. I paid no attention, spoke not a word, and moved on. After traveling some distance, I saw on my right a beautiful dark-haired girl on her bed. I took no notice and kept crawling. When I reached the red light at the end of the tunnel, the master of the lodge met me and told me I was an Oddfellow." (Mr. Raymond Goad told me this tale, but it sounds like one of Uncle Mike's.)

Another of Mike's stories was about a town citizen who liked to drink an extra amount of whiskey and, when he felt himself getting overloaded, would wander off to the cemetary where he could lie down and sleep it off with no one to disturb him. One cold night when he resorted to this plan, he was surprised to find that another drunken man was there and had fallen into a freshly dug grave. Since he couldn't get out, he just lay there on his back moaning, "I am cold . . . I am cold . . . ." The newly arrived drunk looked at him lying at the bottom of the grave and said, "No wonder you're cold, you've kicked all the dirt off of yourself."

Uncle Mike died on January 17, 1986, at Fall River. He was a fine example of a genuine mountaineer who was a faithful, loving family man, a fine craftsman, an entertainer with a good sense of humor, and a true appreciation of his mountain heritage.

My First Funeral

When I was growing up on Lewis Mountain and in the Valley, it always seemed to me that life on the mountain was like being at Jerusalem, the City of God. It was where there was love, joy, and peace! In the Valley, however, I began to see trouble, hurt, and sin and I began to think of it as being more like the city of Jericho than Jerusalem.

When I was about four years old, I began to notice Lee and Clarence, two mentally retarded men who lived in the Valley. I believe they were brothers although they did not really resemble each other except in being retarded. Although both were kind men, Lee seemed to me to have a frightening look, while Clarence had a kind look, sort of like a baby. Both were obedient and would do simple work at home or on big farms (hoeing a garden, for example) where they worked for almost nothing.

I never saw them eat with the family; they were always given a bowl of food and ate on a back porch or under a grapevine. They appeared to be satisfied with whatever was given to them and never asked for anything.

When Clarence died, Aunt Lillie Stoneberger decided to go to the funeral and took me with her. As I walked along with her and others to and from the funeral, I heard the following tales, some of which I knew were true and some I pondered on.

For example, it was said that Clarence would find a secret place in the woods and make him a Personal Musical Instrument in a semi-circle about 50 feet long. He would gather almost every kind of pan, can, pieces of tin, buckets, bottles, and such like from junk piles, take them to the site, and hang them from tree branches with a string or wire. Then he would take two sticks about five feet long and dance and chant a song only he could understand, picking out the rhythm and melody by touching the pans and bottles with the sticks. Not only was the place secret, but Clarence also seemed to have a sixth sense about detecting anyone who came near. In fact, any number of people who had heard him playing his music deep in the woods, tried to slip cautiously under cover and see him perform; when they got there, he was always gone.

It has been said that my Dad, W.B. Stoneberger, was the only person Clarence ever trusted to watch him do his dance and musical show. My Dad reported that his chanting, dancing, and music were amazing and that he just sat there Indian-style and enjoyed the show for an hour.

I have no problem believing this tale because my brother Bill and I were wandering through the woods years after Clarence had died and we ran across his huge musical instrument. We didn't know what it was until much later when someone explained it to us.

Normally, Clarence was a healthy person, but when he was about 50 years old, he got sick and died. It was said that he was not taken into the house during his illness, but was carried to the old chickenhouse and laid on the floor. From there he was facing west where the evening sun was going down. He said, "This is the last time I will ever see that evening sun go down." He died that night.

I wonder if it is possible for a person to be born in this world without love, live a lifetime without love, and die without love? At my first funeral, I said to myself, "Clarence, I am glad you were a friend of my dad. I never did anything for you but come to your funeral, but I believe God in Heaven has prepared a place for you."

The other man, Lee, lived on a number of years. I was walking along a macadam road with some cousins when we came upon about four pair of extremely old, patched, and worn overalls, along with some old shirts and a sweater, in the middle of the road. I asked about it and they said, "Don't you know? It is about the first of June and if Lee has on too many clothes and he gets too hot, he takes some off and throws them away. Then, in the fall of the year, he begins to put more back on."

A story was told of a Lewis Mountain mother who died and left twin infants. They were brought to the Mission Home in hope that someone would adopt them. No one volunteered to take the twins, but after a while a woman said, "I will take the pretty one, but I don't want the ugly one." She took the one of her choice and soon afterwards the other one died. The day of the funeral, the Mission Lady preached a tender, loving message and told how a mother had chosen the beautiful baby; when God in Heaven looked down and saw that the rejected baby was most beautiful, He took this one home to be with Him.

I am glad that at funerals, we can realize that in our hope of life after death, babies, the retarded, the unfortunate, abused, mistreated, and rejected people will get a proper reward.

As a child, I asked Mama what had made Lee and Clarence different from other people. She said, "It may have been nutrition, incest or many things. It wouldn't be good for us to know everything, but we should keep our hearts tender, loving, and forgiving and be like the one in Acts 10:38 who went about doing good."

I had the privilege to work for 43 years in the world's largest rayon plant. About 30 of those years were spent in the powerhouse that burned nearly a thousand tons of coal each day. Here I worked with very influential people, including the town mayor, councilmen, county supervisors, and others. I therefore realize some of the pressures a mayor goes through while trying to live a life of integrity; there are always businessmen who try to use him to make easy money. I realize the strength it takes for public officials not to be used as stooges and to struggle against the pressures to take actions they know are wrong.

As a hillbilly I have been acquainted with the unfortunate from the hills and the leaders of modern society, and I can honestly say that when it comes to eternal life, I would rather cast my lot with the unfortunate who trust in God than to be a king's man and think I had sold my soul to the Devil for the riches of this world.

I have read about a beggar named Lazarus and he made it through all right. I am grateful for my experience in life; I had a terrible dream the night after Clarence's funeral. I dreamed of smothering in a casket in a grave.

I have experienced much misfortune in life, but I think it has all been good for me. I hope to turn all my adversities into triumphs with the help of the good Lord. I also hope I can stand the grinding and burnishing to polish my soul for the Master's use. I believe Clarence did the best he could with what he had to work with and that is what we call a good person.

At my first funeral, I am glad I caught a vision of a loving God who has a city on Mount Zion without sin and he is preparing a place where we are all welcome to come and where there will be love, joy, and peace forever more!

Author's Note: During the many conflicts with American Indians, many died without anyone knowing and many a precious soul rests in an unmarked grave: what a marvelous time Resurrection Day will be!

**The Lewis Mountain School/
Pocosin Episcopal #2 Mission.**

The Lewis Mountain School

On January 3, 1912, John Scott Roach went to the School Board at Stanardsville, Virginia, and asked if they would put a public school on Lewis Mountain. At that time, before the Shenandoah National Park, the peak population of the area, a distance of 105 miles from Waynesboro to Front Royal, was about 5,000. The existing schools were located at the foot of the Blue Ridge Mountains in Rockingham County to the west and in Greene County to the east side, but there was not one on the mountain.

The summers were heavenly in the mountains, with warm, pleasant, sunny days of 80 degrees and nights with cool, soft breezes with a temperature of 60 degrees. But the winters were quite disagreeable with lots of cold, damp days, with temperatures well below freezing, and lots of snow and sometimes blizzards.

Such conditions caused an extreme hardship for the children who had to travel from four to seven miles each way to school. Sometimes sleds pulled by a single horse could be used if equipped with shafts and a breaching harness. If the snow was too deep, however, even this couldn't be used.

The School Board told Grandpa that they were sincerely interested in the education of the mountain children and that they were grateful to him for being the community leader. *But* only so much money had been allocated and ear-marked for the existing schools and there was no way they could help him with a new pioneer school at that time.

Grandpa told them he had a large mountain home they could use as a school free of charge; he would remodel it to their specifications and would furnish the fuel for heat.

The Board replied, "You are more than generous, Mr. Roach. You touch our hearts in the most tender way with your concern for the children's needs and your offer to help. *But* even if you would give us a school building, we know of no teacher who would be willing to go to Lewis Mountain under the extreme hardships she would have to endure there."

Deaconess Carrie G. Makely and the Lewis Mountain School class of 1915-1916.

"Education in our family is a very important thing," Grandpa answered. "I have a daughter who has recently graduated from the seventh grade with high honors. Could she be the teacher?"

After a few moments of silence and talking with Icie, they said, "Mr. Roach, you humble our hearts with your love and concern for the mountain children, plus your great generosity and Icie's willingness to teach. We see no way we could refuse your request."

So a contract was made and Icie Marie Roach would be the first teacher ever to teach at the Lewis Mountain School. According to this document (I have the original), Icie would be paid $15.00 a month, less $1.50 which was to be taken out for the State Teachers' Retirement Fund.

And so it was that early in 1912, the Lewis Mountain School came to birth through a hard and difficult process in the coldest part of the year and at the highest elevation of the Blue Ridge Mountains. Here the doors of knowledge were open to the intelligent minds of the beautiful, healthy mountain children.

As I write about my mountain heritage, a place for Aunt Icie Marie always remains in my heart, because she had character like her parents, John Scott and Cora Roach, and would willingly endure hardship so that others might be blessed. She taught the community children and her own brothers and sisters. My own mother was one of her pupils.

I can imagine seeing Grandpa coming home in the evening from Elkton, with the mule team and the bark wagon, and saying, "Icie Marie! I brought you a newspaper today. There is a current event you will want to teach tomorrow at school." The front-page story recounted the sinking of the Titanic, the greatest passenger ship ever, after it hit an iceberg 95 miles south of the Grand Banks of Newfoundland. A terrible tragedy!

To all my special readers with good mountain blood in their veins and loving spirits, Mama said, "Life is a testing ground. You will hit the D's in life: discouraged, disgusted, disappointed and despondent, but never feel despair. The number one thing to do is purpose good in your heart, use courage, and have faith that love can make a way where there is no way."

The school building was also used as Pocosin Episcopal #2 Mission where Sunday School was taught and Christmas programs enjoyed. I suppose many a child did say, "From Monday until Friday, we would work and play, then back again to Sunday School was where I learned to pray." To many, it was their only school and where the first gates of Heaven were opened, to a hope, and to gain a passport to Eternal life, in a church without a steeple.

One point I would like to make clear. In no way do I wish to imply that there was anything short in the School Board of Greene County in letting a young lady of 14 years of age act as substitute teacher for three or more months until a qualified teacher, probably from the Episcopal Church Headquarters, replaced her.

Mr. E.M. Gibson was Chairman of the School Board, Mr. W.H. Booton was the clerk. These men had great wisdom, along with love and goodness, and measured high in integrity. As a hillbilly, I would say they were clean cut in characters, and as neat, straight, and upright as a Harnesburger's mule's mane.

After fulfilling her contract as a teacher, Icie Marie went to Hagerstown, Maryland, to begin her studies and training to become a registered nurse, which she did. Later she married a fine gentleman named Christopher Panopolis from Greece, who was owner and operator of a restaurant in York, Pennsylvania; Aunt Icie Marie worked as a nurse at the hospital. It was at this location that they lived out their days.

Imagine our delight in going to the mailbox in the Shenandoah Valley during the Great Depression (when many family incomes were less than $100 per year) and finding a big box of goodies from Aunt Icie Marie. This is what I call Blue Ridge Mountain Heritage Love. In good fortune, she would remember us in our misfortune.

I feel it would be appropriate to mention the Great Mystery at this point. Sometime during the years of the Lewis Mountain School, the name Roche got changed to Roach. As we go backward in time from this point, it is always Roche and, as we go forward, it is always Roach. The Great Mystery still remains! We know that Icie Marie used the name Roche when she signed the teaching contract; there are seven gravestones that say the same in Grandpa's family cemetery.

(1987)

John W. Stoneberger 43

Icie M. Roach and her husband, Christopher Panopolis

Butchering Day

As a country boy growing up, there were many days in the year that were special: Christmas, Easter, the first and last days of school, children's day at church with singing and dinner on the ground. Molasses making was always fun, but butchering day was the most interesting.

It is hard to realize now that 90 percent of the people used to make their own living by preparing their own food. Now, only four percent of the people do.

During the 1930s, the years of the Great Depression, we made our living, with the help of a big white horse named Bob, on our little farm. Pork was our main source of meat. We would determine how much hog feed we could afford or raise and so prepare for butchering day a year ahead. At this time, some family incomes were less than $200 per year.

We had a one-horse turn-plow and if we could grow an acre or two of corn, when it got to the roasting-ear stage, we would pull enough to feed the hogs twice a day. If you chop up the ear in the shuck in small pieces, the hogs would eat everything. We would start doing this in July and this would save money, plus carrying feed from the store. For large hogs, you would get your pigs soon after butchering time for next year, but spring pigs would do if you fed them well. A man and his wife could get by with one hog, but most families like three or four to butcher.

Sometimes, meat would get scarce and in October we would butcher a very small hog, if we thought it cool enough to cure the meat. This was always a treat to enjoy the tender, corn-fed meat early in the season. We shared this with neighbors as a rule, since it only lasted until about Thanksgiving, our real butchering day.

It took a week or so to prepare for butchering day. We would take the horse and sled and go to the woods for at least a half cord of good dry hardwood. For small hogs, we sometimes used a 50-gallon barrel to scald in, but for large hogs you had to have a scalding pan or vat and this we would have to borrow from a neighbor. You must have at least two 35-gallon cast-iron kettles, a lard press, a sausage grinder, at least four scrapers to take the hair off, a .22 rifle, and six butchering knives.

In preparing the butchering site, you would want it to be real close to a good spring or stream, because it takes lots of water to scald and wash with. First, you would dig a trench to set your scalding pan over, then put two lengths of old stovepipe on one end of the trench so it would pull a draft on your fire under the pan. The temperature of the scalding water is important and old-timers knew how to do this with a test of the finger: you draw your finger through the water two times and if it is so hot you can't go three times, it is ready; the temperature will be about 160 degrees.

The horse sled, which is about 18 inches high, is parked beside the vat and is used as a work table where you take the hair off after the scald. Two men handle the hogs in the hot water with two chains. After about five minutes of rolling and turning the hog in the scald, he is rolled out on the sled to have the hair scraped off as fast as possible.

From the sled, the hog is then moved to a tripod gallows where he is hung by the tendons of his hind feet. At this place, he got his final cleaning and the head, entrails, liver, and lungs removed. At this time, as a man is working on the hog on the gallows, the next hog is being scalded.

For the next step, you have to have two strong tables, usually made with saw-horses for legs and new lumber or clean butchering boards for tops. Remember, too, that it is at least freezing cold out and cooling starts in the meat during the butchering process. In fact, meat cannot be trimmed until it is cold.

The first hog is moved to one of these tables to be cut up into hams, shoulders, sides, backbone, spareribs, and so forth, with everything going in its proper place: the fat is set aside for lard; lean meat with no skin for the sausage; and headmeat, heart, tongue, kidney, spleen, and liver for the pudding meat.

An unidentified Lewis Mountain boy and a hog.

One man is usually recognized as the top butcher and he is recognized at this point by his being extra clean. He shows his skill by the neat way he trims the meat and how he supervises the many processes that are going on. Everyone's help is needed on butchering day. If you are big enough to roll a peanut, you will be given a job: chunk up the fire, get a fresh bucket of water from the spring, run an errand to the house, get a pan, or bring a knife.

When the last hog is on the gallows, the worst part of the job is over. No one likes getting up at 4:30 in the morning to kill and scald hogs. At the end, the temperature is a little more comfortable and you can take off your galoshes and jacket, wash your hands, and help with the better part.

Hog heads must be cleaned and a boy who could do a good job at this, if he were an Indian, one would say, "Surely he will make a chief!" To do this job, a stake about three feet long is driven into the ground with the sharp end up. The head is set on the stake with the snout up. Now you have to rescald, rescrape, and shave until all is clean. After this, the head is moved to a heavy table where it is cut in half, starting at the mouth and moving toward the neck. The jawbone must be clipped with a wood axe.

The tongue is taken out and the bottom part is sent to the smokehouse to be cured as jowl. The top part is skinned back to the eyes, where the nostril bone is chopped out. With an axe, the head bone is split down through the center and the brains are put in a dish. The eyes, ears, and snout are removed. Now the top piece of the head is ready to be put in the large kettle to be cooked for pudding meat.

Because breakfast was so early, dinner was usually served about 11:00 and we were really hungry. The golden fried tenderloin and liver with brown gravy was always a special on butchering day, along with hot bread, vegetables, pickles, apple or cherry pie, jams and jellies, and plenty of milk, cider and coffee. Mama always served dinner in two shifts, because one group had to be watching the kettles as the others ate.

The heads were the first thing to be put in the pudding kettle to cook in a rapid boil so the meat would turn loose from the bone. Later, the tongues, hearts, kidneys, and livers would be added because they all required less cooking.

About 1:00, after the pudding meat had finished cooking, a second treat of food for the day would be laid out on one of the butchering tables, including very finely sliced pieces of the boiled liver, heart, kidney, tongue, spleen, etc. Everyone was welcome to taste all the different parts to see which was best. Many children did this for the first time.

As the main parts of the meat (hams, shoulders, sides, etc.) were trimmed out and carried to the smokehouse, the backbones and spareribs needed to be chopped up into table-size pieces. This was done with an axe.

Also at this time, someone is checking the sausage meat to remove any skin or too much fat and reduce the large pieces so they will go into the sausage grinder. Boys loved to show off their strength by turning the hand-crank of the sausage grinder as a girl or a woman fed the meat into it. After the sausage was ground, seasoning was added and mixed in. Using the lard press with a special plate attached, the sausage was forced into the casings (made from the small intestine of the hogs). The casings are backed up over the spout so that as the meat fills it, the casing is gradually pulled off the spout. One person controls the shape and size of the sausage while a second person turns the handle of the press. A gallon at a time can be put in the casings.

One of the cast-iron kettles is used to render the fat into lard. The fat is cut into small pieces (about an inch square) and added to the kettle over the fire. The lard must be cooked slowly to render the most lard. You pour the hot grease through the press until it gets full, then you turn the press handle down to a snug pressure. That gives you a cake of cracklings about two inches thick in a gallon container. A small hog will make about a 50-pound can of lard and a large one about two cans. I always loved to eat a few of the freshly pressed cracklings as we made lard. Often we would grind the hot cracklings to be used in making crackling cornbread.

About the time the lard is being rendered, the pudding meat has finished cooking and the kettle is set off of the fire to cool. The bones are taken out and the meat is cut up into pieces small enough to go in the sausage grinder. After the pudding meat has been ground, it is put in gallon stone jars and sealed by pouring a half-inch layer of hot grease from the lard kettle over the top. The jar is set in the cellar with a clean table plate over the top for a lid. The pudding will keep fresh like this for a year or more.

The pudding kettle with the remaining broth (with all the bone slivers removed) is put back on the fire and brought to a boil. Cornmeal, salt, and pepper are added. You stir it and when the mixture gets thick, you take the kettle back off the fire and you have delicious scrapple or pone hoss. If you like it extra rich, a half gallon of pudding can be added to the broth as it boils.

For the next couple of days, there would be more work to do making souse, canning meat, and soap, and then cleaning up. And it was a joy to come home from school hungry and go to the warming closet on the old kitchen range stove where you could load a biscuit with a big fried sausage cake, shoulder ham, or whatever was on the meat platter. You could nibble on it as you went to get the cow or did a chore. I have sat on the river bank fishing for yellow suckers and eaten sandwiches of pork tenderloin on homemade light bread that had been toasted as good as anything I have ever had. It always made me think of butchering day.

I also remember that, as a boy, it was always a pleasure to harness old Bob and hook him to the sled to go borrow butchering equipment from neighbors. It was light work for a horse and he seemed to enjoy the trip. I felt a special joy riding the big horse in the fresh air of the beautiful hills and giving the folks a generous mess of meat when I would take the equipment back to them.

Butchering day was a work day, but a wonderful day of good food and fellowship. Old timers told tales of humor and history that were very interesting. The day also gave us a fresh sense of security knowing that we had a good supply of meat for next year. We could sell extra hams for 20 cents per pound so that we could buy shoes to wear to Sunday School or pigs for the next year.

With 600-800 pounds of meat in the meat house during the Great Depression, you would think, "Butchering these fine hogs is the way to be healthy, wealthy, and wise, because this meat is like old wheat in the mill."

Author's Note: In November of 1992, I helped make apple butter for the benefit of the Bethel Temple Church of God in Front Royal. The ladies of the church held a bazaar at the same time. I suppose the Rev. Jeff Aldridge, the big jolly pastor, should be given credit for planning our delightful day. I know we appreciated Mrs. Peggy Peacher's expertise in the art of making apple butter for directing us and insuring that the final product had the finest flavor.

The apples had been peeled the night before and at 5:30 in the morning the gas burners were torched under the two big 40- and 50-gallon kettles to start the cooking. As the moisture evaporated and the apples cooked down, more prepared apples were added to the kettle and the fire adjusted for the proper boiling point. During the entire day, someone had to stir the kettles with a long-handled wooden stirrer. This keeps an even temperature so the apple butter won't scorch.

The enjoyable part of making apple butter is the conversation and fellowship you find around the kettles. George says, "Isn't this a stirring day?"

I say to Brother Tom Williams, "I can tell you how to stir the kettle: twice around and once through the middle."

"Brother John," he answered, "I was making apple butter before you were born." Even though I was 68, I believe that what he said was true.

We are blessed in our area with orchards that grow such fine apples. Is there anything more pleasant than to walk through an apple orchard in the spring and see the beautiful white and pink blossoms with their fragrant odor or in the autumn to see the trees loaded with fruit from the color of deep green through yellow and gold to deep dark reds?

As I stood by the apple butter kettles as it cooked, smelling the delicious odors, I remember being a boy back on our old farm that sat next to an orchard. In late autumn, you might find a few tree-ripened apples still trying to hold on and these were delicious beyond imagination. The next best thing to it in November is to spread fresh apple butter on waffles or hot buttered toast.

Apple butter is not something anyone makes easy money on. It takes lots of apples, sugar and hard work. We did it to raise money for the church and for the fellowship, the joy of caring and sharing, the fun of making it and that turned a chore into a delightful experience. If you can find a quart of such old-fashioned apple butter for $4 a quart, that would be a bargain. Our 240 quarts sold like hot cakes.

A Heritage of Music

Growing up along the Massanutten at Humes Run, we would often travel the 18 miles from our home in the Valley to Lewis Mountain, the home of my grandparents John Scott and Cora Roche. We went part of the way by car, horse, or mule, but we always had to walk the last part of the steep mountain. Nevertheless, once we got there, it was the joy of our highest expectations.

We, as children, found love in the mountains at its best: the warm welcome, good food, cold water, restful sleep, fresh air, and the peaceful feeling of being loved. There was also lots of singing and music. Jessie Lam, who married our Aunt Lona, played both fiddle and five-string banjo. He taught her to play guitar and she became an excellent singer.

The chambers of my heart ring to this day with the echoes of her sweet voice singing "Bring Back My Blue-Eyed Boy To Me," "The Foggy Mountain Top," and "Don't Give Your Heart to a Rambler Little Girl."

There is a legacy of talent that comes from this area of the mountains. For generations past, the name Lam (or Lamb) has the ability to touch the heart to a depth of joy which has never been touched before, with singing in voices and instruments tuned to perfect harmony in major keys.

I would like to confess to having a question that has passed through my mind. Are all the good times passed and gone because

The banjo playing of Bela Lam (left) is legendary in the mountains; he also owned a grist mill. He is shown in this photograph with his wife (née Rose Meadows), guitarist Alva Lam, and John Paul Meadows.

so many of the old-time entertainers have passed away? This question soon came to an end as the Page Valley Boys Blue Grass Band came on stage at a recent festival with a fine bandleader playing bass, Wesley Gray on the fiddle, Nelson Ray on Dobro, and Greg and Danny Lam singing and playing banjo and guitar.

Tears of joy welled in my eyes as Danny (as lead singer), and Greg harmonizing, sent forth as beautiful a flavor of mountain music as I have ever heard. The musicians in turn would back up the singers in unison of both rhythm and lead, with Greg using both three-finger and claw-hammer style on the banjo, for special original mountain tunes like the Lams have played for generations.

I am proud of our younger generation of musicians who understand their great heritage and the legacy of mountain music. I would like to pay special tribute to the Lams, who have entertained in the Blue Ridge Mountains for generations. With their fine singing and their playing of acoustic instruments, they have carried on this heritage of Blue Ridge Mountain music in its finest form!

The Lewis Mountain Feast

My mother, Elizabeth, was like a flower and just being in her presence was a joy. She had wisdom, understanding, and the gift of holding one's attention when speaking. She found great joy in entertaining with encouraging tales of human goodness.

She often told me of the yearly event that took place at her home on Lewis Mountain when she was growing up. It was called the Mutton Feast and I remember no story she enjoyed telling more than this one.

As you may know, in each American Indian tribe, he who was the strongest in body, soul, and spirit was chief. The mountain people had their clans and each one had its head. This type of government worked well where love brought harmony, harmony brought unity, unity brought power, and everyone was caught up in the benefits.

I am sure Mama felt a touch of dignity because her parents were the heads of the Lewis Mountain clan. Their accomplishments are well worth mentioning because they were very progressive for mountain people in the highest elevations of the Blue Ridge Mountains in the early 1900s.

As I've noted, John Scott Roach hauled bark with a four-mule team to the tannery at Elkton, taking two loads per week for 20 years. The tannery was the largest business in the Shenandoah Valley at that time.

Mountain men peeled the bark from trees for sale to the tannery in Elkton.

The spring of the year, when the sap in the chestnut oak tree began to rise, the bark peeling season would begin. For about six weeks, 60 men would work cutting the trees and taking the bark off with a spud bar. This would produce enough bark for two loads per week for the full year. As a result, there was a monthly payroll for the men of Lewis Mountain.

Mr. J.L. Armentrout, who owned both the Shenandoah Tourist Home and a large river-bottom farm on the road between Elkton and Shenandoah, paid Mr. Roach 50 cents per head a month to pasture 150 head of cattle on the Lewis Mountain grass land during the grazing season.

This cash income was a great help for Mama's family and, as noted above, provided for the Lewis Mountain School and the Mission built onto their home. It also paid one man's wages to work on the roads year round, building water breaks and filling in the flash-flood wash-outs. All of the Lewis Mountain roads were private, rough, steep, and in constant need of attention; there were no public roads until the construction of the Skyline Drive.

As Grandpa looked over a year of progress, there was much to be thankful for, so at the end of bark-peeling season and with summer on its way, it was time for the mountain community to gather at the Lewis Mountain farm of John Scott Roach for a Mutton Feast and a full day of rest and fellowship.

A full-grown sheep had been selected months before, and was stall-fed to prime condition on grain, hay, and good cold spring water. Early in the morning of the feast day, the animal was butchered and put in a large cast iron kettle and cooked good and tender for the noon meal. Other things like fresh cole slaw in three-gallon dish pans and baked foods were also prepared.

Some people consider mountain people poor by some standards. It is true they had little money, but don't forget the great natural resources of the bountiful mountains. John Scott Roach was one who understood these things and he could feed 200 people a delightful meal in one day with no strain. And he considered it a great pleasure.

Cora Virginia Roach, his wife (we called her Grannie), was well accustomed to feeding large numbers. I remember her springhouse where large amounts of cold food were stored. In the spring of the year, when her milk cows were in a heavy flow of milk, she would churn lots of butter, put it in pound-size blocks with her printer, and store it in five- or ten-gallon stone crocks in the cool spring house. When the need would arise to use large amounts, she would rinse off the salt with cold water and it would be fresh and delicious. Corn hominy, sauerkraut, and salt fish were also kept in the spring house.

She lived to see how much she could help or give. The mountain people showed her much gratitude and one professional minister left in print that the food she served in dish pans was more delicious than some he had eaten off of silver in rich estates where there was mistrust.

Food was one of the things that helped make Feast Day a great day of enjoyment, but there were many other things I remember. Young mothers and fathers showed off new babies, children searched for old friends and made new friends. There was the excitement of new romance, or marriages. Older men and women formed their circles of interest. Many games were played, always including wrestling. After the food, games, talking, contests, singing, and wrestling, there would be a story or tale told by the chief of the clan. All would listen and John Scott Roach once told this one:

"I had a musket rifle and a good pack of dogs and was hunting near Lost River over in West Virginia. The dogs had put a huge buck deer on the run. After several shots, I had wounded the animal bad and he went down to a little basin and refused to run. Here the deer decided to fight the dogs with hoof and horn.

"The musket was a great rifle. It would shoot hard and hit almost anything except what you would aim at. With the dogs all around the deer, I was afraid to shoot at it for fear of missing and hitting a dog. I decided to sit the rifle against a tree and take my large, very sharp hunting knife and go in to finish off the badly wounded deer.

"I went in and grabbed the deer by its large horns, but it had unbelievable strength and threw me around in many directions. After many tries and almost exhausted, I finally made the kill. Then it dawned on me what a foolish, dangerous thing I had done to try to kill such a large deer in this fashion!

"With sweat dripping off of my face, I walked a few steps to surmise the situation. I was talking to myself and I said, 'Oh yeah, old fellow! I can see this is your old fighting ground! I can see that old snag on the tree about ten feet off the ground and that old pair of faded, patched-up overalls hanging there. I guess you must have killed a man here some time ago!'

"I reached for my hip pocket to get my big red handkerchief to wipe the sweat from my face. And could you believe it? I had no pants on. Those were my pants hanging on the snag that I had lost while fighting that deer!"

After much laughter, Mr. Roach would ask the Reverend Frank Persons, the Episcopal minister, to come forward and offer prayer, praise and benediction for the day. He would also remind everyone to keep love in their hearts, to support the school and Mission with attendance, and to look forward to another Mutton Feast next year.

Children's Day

Another special day was Children's Day, an annual, all-day service held at the Methodist Church in Jollett Hollow. I remember driving in a Model T Ford with my family up Naked Creek Road to the foot of the mountain to attend. I believe I was about six years old, so it would have been the summer of 1930.

Having never been to this event before, I remember feeling awkward and bashful when play time arrived. I was at a complete loss as to what to do or how to fit into the festivity of the children's play. I sat down on a big rock on the lawn and pretended to be happy as I watched the children run and play with hearts full of joy. In truth, I was as lonesome as a homesick mouse under a hog pen floor on a dark and stormy night.

I had been sitting there on the rock for about 10 minutes, wondering how to meet the other children, when suddenly something went over my eyes. I thought someone had blindfolded me. Before I had time to suffer much apprehension, the beautiful voice of a young girl said, "Guess who?" I said, "I don't know." She removed the blindfold – actually the red ribbon she had been wearing in her hair.

To my surprise, the girl with the red ribbon was the one I had so admired for the last 10 minutes as she played with the children and ran so effortlessly across the lawn with her dark hair floating in the breeze. I was amazed that she could slip behind me so quietly and delighted to know that she had welcomed me into the fun with such a clever gesture of friendliness. I do know she opened a door of love to a lonely boy's heart at a mountain church Children's Day Meeting that will last forever.

The Reverend Frank Persons, the Episcopal minister who lived in the John Scott Roach home for years and preached on Lewis Mountain

Mountain Moonshine Whiskey

As I write of my mountain memories, I speak of things that my mother has told me, as well as things I have experienced. For example, Mama said that a gallon jug of moonshine whiskey with rock candy in it was always on the mantelpiece over the fireplace in the living room in the home where she was raised on Lewis Mountain.

This custom was part of our way of life and everyone could use it of their own free will. I have heard her say many a time, "Where it came from I don't know, but one thing for sure; when the level dropped within a couple inches of the bottom of the jug, it would fill up again. It appeared we used very little of it, and many a time it seemed to do much good."

A traveler or stranger was often given a drink. The young men in the family sometimes took a drink when coming home cold or wet from hunting. The minister who lived in the home mission would sometimes take a small nip before taking his Sunday evening nap. But Mama said, "When I grew up and went out into the world and saw the abuse of alcohol, then I hated the stuff."

A man of wisdom once said, "A man should never drink strong drink; if a king who has the queen, horses and gold got drunk, he would cry because no one loved him. And if a lazy, worthless beggar was given a strong drink, he would feel like a king."

So, strong drink stirs the emotions of men and can be artificial sadness or happiness. If we have love in our hearts, if we work and pray, if we give and do good, we find the joy of life and this is the real thing.

Mama believed that the Blue Ridge mountaineer came as close to knowing how to use whiskey as anyone ever did and so his moonshine served a useful purpose on Lewis Mountain. Grandpa considered it a necessity in his home, because he delighted in being a man of hospitality and this was one of his ways of being a servant of God. Grandpa died in 1917 and I suppose the jug went empty, dried up, and disappeared.

But I remember very well the summer of 1928. I was four or five years old and we were on our way up the Naked Creek road to the old home place. We stopped at a special Aunt's home on the left before we came to the top of the mountain and here she gave me the honor of carrying a half-pint bottle of yellow corn liquor as we walked the last two miles to Grannie Roche's place. The small bottle would take the place of the faithful old jug that had been on the fireplace mantelpiece for years and years.

Like everything else, there was a special art in knowing how to make good moonshine whiskey or brandy. The whiskey was made from grain and the brandy from fruit. The mountain people used less sugar, but very pure water, clean equipment, and good ash wood for slow distilling.

I have friends in both Virginia and Tennessee who make a little mountain dew just to remember the old days. I like to take the caps off of the bottles and smell the brandies and whiskies. I think rye whiskey has the most clean and distinct odor of all.

I once knew a beautiful young lady and someone asked her if she had ever had any moonshine. She smiled very cheerfully and said, "Yes, I have and I learned one thing: it must be used with moderation or you might start talking back to your Daddy."

A man who was real drunk was walking with a friend across a high river bridge at night and saw the reflection of the full moon in the water. He asked his companion, "What is that I see in the water like a huge cake of butter?" His friend replied, "That's the moon." The drunken man answered, "If that is the moon down there, what in the world are we doing up here?"

Grandpa lived on the sunny side of the mountain and that is what I like to write about, but we know there is a dark, cold side, too. And this next story, from the trouble side of life, is the saddest I ever heard and it has been in my memory since early childhood.

A beautiful, young mountain mother with a family of small children was shot and killed by her drunken, jealous husband. It was behind their little cornhouse that the awful deed was done. When neighbors found her, the children were gathered around the mother and one of the little girls was trying to feed the crying and hungry infant baby from the dead mother's breast. The father and husband was sent to prison for life. Last year, I was traveling with a cousin near Wolftown, Virginia, and she pointed out a building along the road and said, "Do you remember when we were kids and the man killed his wife on the mountain? They brought the body down here on a mule sled so that the undertaker could take care of her."

Somewhere along the road of life, I lost the desire to drink strong drink and now have no taste for alcohol. But, I do have an appreciation for all the good it has done.

Aunt Josie Stoneberger told me this next story. A family was terrible sick with the whooping cough. My dad, W.B. Stoneberger, was asked to ride a horse to the town of Shenandoah to get medicine for them from the doctor. The river bridge had been washed out by a flood and, as he was trying to find a fordable way across the river, his horse slipped on a slick rock and fell, throwing him into the cold river! He rode the rest of the way, about three miles, and when he came in the house, his clothes were froze on him, because the night air was so cold in late November.

They heated the stove the best they could and put him in dry clothes in the living room bed. They packed the small children around him to help get him warm, but he still shook so bad he almost shook the bed apart! Then Aunt Josie gave him a hot toddy of moonshine whiskey and ginger. This broke the chill in a few minutes and he didn't as much as get a bad cold from all the exposure.

Moonshine whiskey has been put to many good uses by God-fearing people; on the other hand, everyone must beware of its wrong uses. I once heard a discouraged drunken man say,

> Oh, Whiskey, you villain,
> You've been my downfall,
> You've beat me and banged me
> And robbed me of all.

That Mule and Me

Grandpa John Scott Roach said, "The mule is by far the best animal for the bark wagons in the mountains. They are strong, tough in both heat and cold, sure-footed, easily broken to harness and, for a little love and fair treatment, they would gladly give you a full day's work for shelter, clean water, eight ears of corn, and a good fork of hay." And his mules were very handsome animals with their 1200-pound, stocky bodies, fine posture with heads held high, manes and tails trimmed to perfection, and feet well shod.

I have heard it said, "Grandpa may dress in a faded blue shirt and a well-worn pair of overalls with a few patches here and there, but his wagons were well greased and maintained and his four-mule team was a picture of health, and strength, in harness of good quality, oiled leather."

The rainfall in the mountains is much more than the Valley, being as much as 36 inches per year. Since the team worked six days per week, they went through many showers on the road. Under the hard leather collar of the harness was about two inches of thick padding. This was used to cushion and protect the shoulders of the mule from pain, bruises, and soreness, since that was where the greatest pressure was put when pulling. If the padding got wet from rain, it could cause the mule's shoulder to rub raw and make a red, ugly, and painful sore that could leave a scar.

These mules were loved like one of the family and everyone was concerned with their good welfare. For instance, about once a year, when Grandpa would butcher a beef, Grandma would very carefully tan the hides which were then used to make the housing that formed the collars on the mule harnesses. The collars were tailored so the brass knobs on the harness went through two holes in the housing to hold it firmly in place and thus keep the padding dry. This and much else was done to insure the comfort and protection of these valuable animals; they pulled the heavy loads 15 miles to town, but they also brought back money for Grandpa, tea for Grandma, and candy for the kids.

The mountaineer enjoyed few luxuries. The Singer sewing machine and Victrola (a record player) were two of the first modern machines to play a part in his humble, joyful life – if he was well off enough to afford them. The mule did much in helping to bring these items to a few mountain homes.

In 1916, the prosperous, happy Roach family of Lewis Mountain suffered a terrible loss when John Scott Roach died at 67 years of age. Now, the bark wagons would roll no more and the mules would not be put again into harness. The mules stood almost in formation in the pasture near the spring house, overlooking the main house and garden, as Grandpa was placed in his final resting place in the family graveyard, near the garden where the lilacs and roses bloom.

With much regret, a sale soon took place and anxious buyers came to haggle over a price for the prestigious mule team and equipment. One mule, Coley, "drew the short straw" and was allowed to remain and retire on the Lewis Mountain homeplace, she being the oldest, best looking, and good-natured; she was also so faithful and obedient in her work as a team or single-line leader that even a woman or a youth could use her for work in the garden.

Coley had been one of the wheel-horse mules that had pulled the bark wagons for some 20 years, but now she whiled away her days in the 90 acres of lush, bluegrass pasture field with plenty of shade and cold spring water.

Grandma wrote to Elizabeth, my mother, in the Valley and said, "If you have any need for Coley, I will send her over by Jessie." Upon mother's reply, she did just that. Coley plowed the peach orchard and garden and even such small work was done lovingly and cheerfully. With these chores completed, however, there was nothing for her to do. After about a week of idleness, she up and disappeared. The loss of Coley distressed and worried us, so we watched the sky for buzzards (in case she had wandered off and died) and looked for tracks to see which way she might have left the farm, but we found no sign of her.

A letter came from Grandma and she said, "Elizabeth, we went out to the barn to feed the animals this morning and there was Coley in her stall. We don't even know how she got there!" Oh, what good news to know Coley was safe at home. But many questions were left unanswered in our minds. We knew that mules have a dislike for rivers and bridges, so how did she travel those 20 miles home? Did she travel cross-country, jumping fences and swimming rivers, or did she go on roads and use the bridges over the Shenandoah River?

You can rate a mule's intelligence any way you like, but Coley knew there was no better place on earth than her Blue Ridge mountain home. There is something that draws my heart, just like Coley's, to the very same house (now only a foundation), spring, and graveyard, where I pray and find a special blessing in my soul.

I believe Grandpa lived the best mountain life of all ages, about 50 years of it on Lewis Mountain, with its abundant resources and few restrictions. It was a place where love was the law that ruled.

As I think about the valuable mountain mule, its true worth, the roll it played in history, a recitation by George Brenner comes to my mind. It goes something like this:

"When I was a boy growing up, there was a man we called Old Rivers who worked a big black mule named Midnight. Old Rivers was a friend of mine. He would plow those rows long and straight and I would walk behind him and bust up those clods with my own bare feet.

"If Midnight began to get hot, he would rest him a few minutes in the shade. He would take a big red handkerchief out of his pocket and wipe his cheerful face and bald head and say, 'Boy! One of these days, I'm going up where the cotton grows tall, the corn is green, and those fields you don't have to plow!'

"I grew up and left home; I had been gone for some time when one day I got a letter from Mama. It said:

Dear Son, You know your Dad and I are getting older, and we are concerned with our wandering boy. We go to our little church every Sunday and pray you can find the peace for your heart you are searching for, and the road that leads back home. And by the way, your good friend Old Rivers died last week. There were quite a few at his funeral.

When I read those words, I dropped to my knees in deep remorse and prayed: 'Dear God in Heaven, forgive me of my many sins, guide me on your righteous pathway and help me to lead others in your way.' As the spirit of forgiveness swept over me and the joy of Salvation entered my heart, I rose to my feet and said, 'One of these days, I am going to climb that mountain! I'm going up where the cotton grows tall, the corn is green, and those fields you don't have to plow! Old Rivers, that mule, and me.' "

An unidentified mountain man with a mule in harness

The Treasure Hunt

Aunt Lonie Lam once said, "John, let's you and I go on a treasure hunt on Lewis Mountain one day!" Then she told me this story.

One mile from the Skyline Drive at the Bear Fence going east down Slaughter Road is the Devil's Ditch Stream. In the early 1900s there was a small cabin on the left just after you crossed the stream. It sat on a little knoll just barely big enough for the cabin and a tiny garden. The wagon road ran between the knoll and the steep mountain, leaving the road for the front yard and a steep drop off behind the cabin.

At the cabin lived a nice lady named Jennie Morris. It seemed that everyone loved her. She was neat and trustworthy and grew a beautiful garden. It was rather unusual for a single woman to live alone in the mountains.

A well-loved young man named Joe Samuels worked for Grandpa John Scott Roche for years maintaining the private mountain roads, making water breaks, filling in washouts after heavy rains, and so forth. One cold winter night he was found dead a short distance west of Jennie's cabin, lying on the Slaughter Road. The true reason of his death was never known; some reckoned he had a stroke, while others thought he had drunk too much, went to sleep, and froze to death.

Jennie had been gone from her home for several days and, since no doors were locked in the mountains, the man who found Joe carried him to Jennie's cabin and laid him on her bed. The next morning, he returned with a mule and sled and took the body away.

When Jennie returned and heard the news about a dead man spending the night in her bed, she was very disturbed. She said, "I'll never spend another night in that cabin!"

Jennie asked Aunt Lonie, who was nine years old at the time and lived nearby, to come over that very day. She needed to confide in Lonnie and to ask a favor of her before leaving her home.

A well-to-do businessman from the Valley had come up in the summer to do work at the W.B. Stoneberger sawmill, a short distance downstream at Franklin Spring. He had asked Jennie to take care of two pistols and two expensive gold watches for him while he worked at the mill. He had not returned yet for his possessions and, unfortunately, she only knew his name but not his address or any way to contact him. She had, therefore, wrapped the man's valuables in cloth, put them in a heavy metal box, and buried it under her porch.

"Lonie," she said, "if he ever comes back to inquire of me, tell him where I put his things, but don't you ever tell anyone about this secret." She kissed Lonie, shed a tear, and said, "I am leaving my little home now, and I never expect to come back. So, good-bye Lonie and God bless you!"

The little cabin grew old, rotted, and fell down. Aunt Lonie carried the secret in her heart for more than 50 years and told me the story. A few years later, she died, before we had a chance to take our treasure hunt. I remember the story, however, every time I pass the location of the Jennie Morris cabin. What I really like about the story was Jennie's beautiful character: she had rather deposit those treasures in the Blue Ridge Mountains for safekeeping than to take something that belonged to someone else. She also put her trust in a loving child to carry out her request.

Old-time mountain people talk of the sadness of Joe's death. Carrie Mackley, the teacher at St. Andrews Roche Mission made note of Joe's death in her diary in 1916. Many people regretted that Jennie was spooked to despair and left her home by a man showing kindness for his dead friend.

There seems to be something about the mountains that is mystifying in both sunshine and darkness; it seems the sunshine is more pleasant and the nights darker. If you could imagine spending a day at Jennie's old cabin site, you could walk under the huge hemlock trees on a heavy carpet of thick needles. Here, Mama, as a young girl, used to catch rainbow trout with stickworm bait. They would flash in the morning sunshine in the clear crystal white water. Beautiful butterflies floated over the gorge and big bumblebees bumbled over the heavy dew-covered flowers. But at night, in the dark of the moon, it gets as black as a wolf's mouth in that hollow. Foxes bark and tree limbs rub together under great pressure making sounds like groans of misery or death. As the stream goes over the falls, gurgling rhythms fill the air and every cricket or bug seems to have a fiddle in the grass. There is something about the environment of the mountains that can cause you to have a mythological imagination and play tricks with your mind. Knowing these things, you can perhaps better understand what brought Jennie to the mountain and why she left.

My brother Bill did well for himself as a worker and businessman. He married a wealthy lady and they enjoyed travelling the world in search of precious stones, whether in the field or from haggling merchants in exotic markets. I'd be the first to admit that pigeon-blood ruby and star sapphires are beautiful, but the real jewels I love best are in mountain memories in the Blue Ridge Mountains like Aunt Lonie Lam, Jennie Morris, and Joe Samuels. We should never stop searching for treasure, but we should always remember that the Pearl of Great Price is the greatest of all.

The Teamster and the Bees

I have always loved horses and thought they were beautiful, useful, and intelligent animals. I have also observed the men who handle horses or mules and have been amazed at the things a good teamster can do with a well-trained team. There is much to know about being a good teamster. A man must know what a team can do and how to train them to perfection for the difficult task, by soft, gentle signals or sharp, stern commands.

Sewell Collier was a farmer all his life and retired in a comfortable home in Charlottesville. I would often sit on his porch and listen to him review the past. He once said, "I have owned some nice vehicles in my life, but never have I driven anything that gave me as grand a feeling as getting on my wagon seat, knowing I was in command of a well-matched team of horses, eager to respond to the slightest touch of the reins or a soft command."

He, along with others, worked horses and hauled much wood from the Lewis Mountain area. To get out of the hollow, one had to travel several miles on a route shaped like a U. There was one other way to get out: 200 yards up an extra steep mountain to a main road. This road did not zig-zag or rattlesnake like most steep mountain roads do. It may have come into use as an old log road which went straight up the mountain. There was a hazard on this steep road: a smooth limestone rock about 10-feet long that lay the full width of the road.

A typical mountain bark wagon

Uncle Dick is the only teamster I have ever known who could take a four-horse team and pull a full cord of green wood up this steep an incline over the smooth rock. Other teamsters were afraid to do this, knowing that a well-shod horse can't pull on slick rock. Of course, if you cause a horse to slip and fall, it could break a leg.

To see Uncle Dick pull this mountain and demonstrate the skill of a teamster and the power of his horses was amazing. He would pull the first 100 yards, stop, and chock the wagon to let the horses catch their breath. This was maybe 30 feet from the rock. Then, with a sharp, rash command, he would call on the full team to do their stuff. With as much speed as the team could gain to hit the rock, he would pull in the leaders with the reins and call for the wheel horses to strain. The leaders would walk cautiously over the slick rock as the wheel horses pulled with all their might. Then the leaders could see where they could get their front feet on dirt and they would sort of rear up and come down hard with their front shoes, pulling with their front feet to help move the load. As soon as both leaders had all four feet on dirt, the teamster would call the sharp command for them to bear the load while the wheel horses walked across the rock. Then all four horses would again pull together and move the load forward.

A teamster's skill was demonstrated at pulling this steep mountain in seven or eight minutes, which would take an hour or so to go around. Uncle Dick pulled his horses harder than any teamster I ever saw, yet I never knew of him to injure a horse.

In the days before the Civil War, when the old South enjoyed the good days of splendor, there was a planter with a lovely estate in good production and happy, contented workers. He would also have a teamster who drove his team and carried him about in his carriage, on business and for social and other events. The old gentleman was delighted because his teamster was so congenial and happy. He would whistle or sing softly with excellent rhythm and seemed to have a way of instilling this in the horses.

After prayer, breakfast, and small general orders on the plantation, he could look forward to the daily trip in his carriage as the most enjoyable part of his day. Here he found peace of mind, rest, and relaxation and made his best decisions. He would hear the soft voice of the teamster as he sang:

> The Lord He can set your heart to dancin'
> The Lord He can thrill you through & through
> The Lord He can set your heart to dancin'
> And set your feet to dancin', too.

He noticed the way the teamster held the reins in his left hand, as his feet would tap a soft drum-like sound and his right hand would keep a double-time rhythm on the carriage seat. The horses would fall into a rhythm of their own, with snorts through their noses and moving their heads and manes in the wind. Their feet would move and set the jingle of the harness to the teamster's rhythm. Sometimes the teamster would whistle the familiar melody, sing again and change the words:

> The Holy Ghost can set your heart dancin'
> The Holy Ghost can thrill you through & through
> The Holy Ghost can set your heart dancin'
> And set your feet to dancin', too.

A team of horses held by an unidentified mountain man.

The planter watched as the driver took a long whip and pulled a horse fly off of the lead horse without disturbing the animal. One day, he put his head outside the carriage and said, "Jake, there is a big hornet's nest on a tree we are soon going to pass. Could you take your whip and cut it off as we go by?"

Jake said, "No, sir. Those bees are organized and if they don't bother me, I don't want to bother them!" Sometimes a good servant does have the wisdom of a king.

John Scott Roach was a teamster in the Blue Ridge Mountains for more than 50 years and he said, "The bee is the most dreaded thing the teamster could ever face during the hot months of summer." And he told this story.

Jerry, one of his most congenial children, learned to love work and responsibility at a tender age. After he was a well-developed man and considered one of the best teamsters in the area, this happened. He had a four-mule team and was hauling a load of bark up a mountain. As he came near the top of a ridge, he called the team to a halt so they could catch their wind and let their breathing slow down. Unfortunately, the mules had stopped over a nest of yellow-jackets on the road and the sound of their feet had caused the bees to stir a counsel of war. They soon began to sting the mules in the most sensitive places! The team was suddenly frightened into a stampede and it appeared that their idea was to run into the woods to escape rather than to stay on the road. As the lead mules would try to go left, then right, the wagon wheel ran behind a four-foot hickory tree stump and stalled the team.

As the leaders began to kick violently at the wheel horses, Jerry decided he had to act. He secured the reins and, using a sharp teamster's axe, tried to chop several deep cuts in the hickory to weaken the tree. He then intended to get back on the wagon and let the team pull and finish breaking the tree; he would be able to control the team again once they were a safe distance from the bees.

Before he could get back on the wagon, however, the team broke loose and ran away without him. He followed them for a mile or so. When he found the exhausted mules, he was dismayed to find that one of the leaders had got tangled in the harness, fallen, and been dragged to its death under the wagon. This was the saddest moment a Lewis Mountain teamster could ever experience.

Author's Note: I can imagine seeing the Captain of the Host, speaking for the Queen Bee, saying, "We are the Yellow Jackets and we are organized. Lewis Mountain is the land of milk and honey and we, with authority, will rule this domain! We were victorious in today's battle and all who fought underneath did a good job.

"Special recognition is due to those who did attack the eyes and ears of the leader mules. One 1,200 pound mule was blinded in her run, fell in her harness, and was dragged to death. We Bees have suffered no losses, and stand strong in our full number and weight of one ounce and two grams each for our full nest.

"Now hear this! All who took part in the battle today, feel free to take the rest of the day off. Wet your feet in the cool, clear waters of Devil's Ditch Stream. Or fly to the Crest of Bear Fence Rock and enjoy the scenery of the world. Or lay in the sweet smelling laurel blossoms and rest. But everyone be ready to report for duty at sunrise, because tomorrow is another day. Thank you all for a job well done."

(1988)

Queenie the Mule

As I've mentioned, Lewis Mountain is centrally located in the Shenandoah National Park, with Rockingham and Greene counties dividing it east and west along the crest of the mountain. A road near Bear Fence Mountain divides it north and south. There is a park fire road going east called Slaughter Road. Going west to Route 340, there is a road running parallel with Naked Creek called Naked Creek Road.

Near the foot of the mountain along Naked Creek is a village of about 200 people called Jollett Hollow. A fine gentleman named Van Taylor, who had the honor of being Justice of the Peace for a long time, lived here and owned a mule named Queenie.

After the tannery at Elkton was destroyed by a disastrous fire, bark-hauling from the mountains came to an end. At the same time, sawmilling was slow and so there was little work for Queenie.

In the Jollett Hollow area, grassland was scarce and so Mr. Taylor took the liberty of letting Queenie graze along the roads of the community. Queenie would wander about freely during the day and come back home at night. This went on for some time and she soon found all the choicest spots, including many special lawns and gardens which were unfenced and where the grass was good and the vegetables delicious. Needless to say, this caused an awful lot of discontent among the residents, but they where afraid to voice any complaint because Queenie's owner was also the lock, stock, and barrel of the Jollett Hollow law enforcement system and everyone wanted to get along with him.

Queenie's heavenly leisure soon became such a torment that the villagers declared war on her and would pelter her with rocks whenever they thought she was going too far. As time went on the situation grew worse and soon boys were looking for any chance to hit her with a stone and watch her run. At first, Queenie tried to find a way to escape, but she must have soon realized that running was not the answer because she was still peltered as she ran.

One day, after a painful stone struck her, she looked and saw the second stone coming. As her temper was rising, she wheeled, kicked, and batted the stone with her hind foot in the direction of the boys, almost hitting one of them. After this, she had a little more peace of mind because the boys soon learned she could "bat" rocks about as well as they could "pitch" and so they threw fewer rocks at her.

One day, she was grazing in a nice little garden when Mrs. Ida Meadows threw a rock at her. Unfortunately, Queenie saw the rock coming, wheeled and kicked, batting the rock back at the woman and causing a bad injury. The sad news of the incident reached the ear of Mr. Taylor who took pride in being a law-abiding citizen. He didn't want this to happen again. He also knew that he would be at fault if he continued to let this rock-batting mule wander at large and someone were killed. And so he put Queenie up for sale. Unfortunately, this was at a time when money was hard to come by and mule sales were slow.

Uncle Virgie Lam, a peace-loving man, heard the story and offered to do what he could to help the Justice of the Peace and the folks of Jollett Hollow by taking this dangerous mule away. He traded a good supply of apples for Queenie and took her up to his large mountain farm near Devil's Jump where she would be out of the way and could live in peace.

Here she enjoyed the good life with good food, mountain spring water, and a trip to the store once in a while. The two got along for some time until one day she lashed out with her back foot for some unknown reason and kicked Uncle Virgie in the chest, knocking him down! He said, "The force of the kick was almost spent before it hit or it would have killed me." Even then, the mule shoe put a powerful dent in the heavy nickel case of the antique Elgin watch that he was carrying in the bib of his overalls.

This caused Virgie to be afraid of the mule and so he gave her to his son-in-law, Johnnie Lam. Johnnie, as soon as apple-picking season was over, built her a nice little stable all her own. It was not long, however, until one day when he went to get Queenie and she came out, wheeled, and kicked the new door off the stable with both hind feet. And so now Johnnie was afraid of her too and traded her off for a used cook stove.

About this time, the Shenandoah National Park was taking possession of the mountain land and Johnnie Lam had to move to a homestead property in the Valley. The stove was left in the mountains, considered worthless due to the grates being burned out. Years later, he went back to get it for an antique, but it was gone. This was as far as we could trace the life of Queenie the mule.

I feel Queenie was a good mule who had been abused in life. What a shame this had to happen and only because her character was so deformed by mistreatment. I feel sure she could have kicked at a football game.

(1989)

Author's Note: My little Blue Ridge Mountain Mother used to say, "It is really not the bad things in life that causes all the trouble; the main source is a lack of love."

Beyond the Blue Mountains

I was reluctant to write this tale. It has some merits and some things I am ashamed of, yet I need to be honest as I write about the history of Lewis Mountain. My folks were the community leaders who put the first mission and school there. I know of negative things that did happen and it is my personal opinion that this tale bears much truth and some imagination.

I was born on Lewis Mountain but raised in the Valley at Humes Run. Our home was in-between two country stores and two churches: the C.M. Dovel store and St. Peter's to the north and the W.H. Alger store and Bethel Church to the south.

As children, we went to both stores and both churches. For some reason, we bought more groceries at Alger's store, even though it was much further to carry them. As a boy, I often wondered if it was because we used a charge account there; whenever we paid a good amount, Mr. Alger always gave us a huge bag of penny candy, really good!

On our way to Bethel Church or Alger's store, during the Great Depression, we would pass through Greenwood, an all black community of about 200 people. This is where we first heard the following tale.

Mr. Habard Willis lived near the center of this village in one of the few painted houses. His place was well cared for, with a nice lawn grazed short, a small garden, and fruit trees blossomed with plenty of shade. He seemed to be a kind man who would allow the village children to gather at his home after he had done his morning chores. As the summer sun got hotter, he would entertain the young folks with stories and tales. Once, when my brother Bill was on his way home from Alger's store with a load of groceries or hog feed on his back, he decided to stop for a short rest in Greenwood. He was right by the Willis house and he saw that Mr. Willis was getting into his daily act of feeding the hungry minds of the blessed children who loved to hear him speak. So, Bill stayed and listened, too.

The Massanutten Mountains are about a mile west of Greenwood and the Blue Ridge Mountains quite a distance east. One of the children with an eager mind to learn asked, "What is way over there beyond those Blue Mountains?"

Mr. Willis smiled, chuckled, and said, "Well, I have been over there and I can tell you."

"I once agreed to trade a mule of excellent quality to Mr. John Scott Roach for a beautiful fine riding horse. To do this, I had to take the mule over and bring the horse back. So it took one day to go over to those Blue Mountains and the next day to come back.

"Mr. Roach owned over 1,000 acres of land, a well-built log home and barn and a strong mule team. He was a very congenial mountaineer with a large, well-respected family, well . . . well . . . all except one son named Josh who seemed to have an extra amount of energy and mischief.

"The evening I got there, Mrs. Roach sent me a huge plate of food by one of the children out to the barn and it was as delicious as I ever tasted. I prepared myself a soft bed in the sweet-smelling hay and settled down for the night.

"I was sleeping like a log when sometime during the night, Josh came out, woke me up, and said, 'Say, fellow, can't you dance?'

"I could see he was in the mood for a frolic or a fight and so, very polite, I says, 'Why yes, I can hit a couple of steps.' He said to come with him and he headed toward the main house. In the large living room, he poured me a drink of mountain dew from a gallon jug and took one himself. He then started playing a five-string banjo like his fingers were on fire and my feet were clicking on the heavy plank floor in rhythm, note for note as he played!

"When daylight came, Mrs. Roach came down from upstairs with a look of bewilderment on her face. She looked at me and said, 'What in the world do you think you are doing?'

"I nodded my head and pointed at Josh with the banjo, the jug of dew, and a pistol! Then she said, 'You stop that dancing right now! Josh, I am ashamed of your behavior. Don't you ever let this happen again!'"

At this part of the story, Mr. Willis had the perfect attention of his listeners. He raised both hands to emphasize the punch line and said, "That was one time in my life I danced all night long."

The children all broke into a joyful laughter. Then one asked, "Mr. Willis, did you really dance all night long?"

Mr. Willis answered, "Yes, sir . . . yes, sir . . . I really did!"

As more laughter broke out, he said, "No . . . no . . . no, you would never want to go beyond those Blue Mountains, unless you feel you could dance all night!" More laughter broke out and there was much mumbling and talking, with a few saying they believed they could dance all night.

At the end of the story, Bill said he smiled, put his load on his shoulder, and started walking toward home. He says he thought to himself, "I sure hope they don't know Josh is my uncle or I might have had to dance all day! I do know one thing, they will never find out by me telling them!"

Bill was a strong, handsome boy and many a Sunday morning he was the admiration of many a Greenwood youth as he walked barefoot to Bethel Church Sunday School. He was most likely wearing a beautiful, blue-striped shirt that my precious mother had made from the clothes of her dead brother, who was Uncle Josh.

Uncle Josh died working in the coal mines as a young man and is buried on Lewis Mountain in the family grave-yard. He drew the largest funeral ever to take place there.

I believe Mr. Willis was a loving, forgiving man and he will be blessed. I remember those Sunday mornings as most precious, traveling with Mama, our spiritual leader, walking over rocks, roads, under hot sun, owning almost absolutely nothing, yet dressed well and feeling like young princes as we went through Greenwood on our way to church. There we learned of Someone who owns cattle on a thousand hills, also the potatoes under the hills, and that He loves us all and all men should love one another in the Valley and beyond the Blue Mountains. (1990)

Family Tree of John W. Stoneberger

	Paternal Line	*Maternal Line*
Grandparents:	Hyram Stoneberger Lola Dovell Turner	**John Scott Roche** **Cora Virginia Keckley Reynolds**
Parents:	**William B. Stoneberger**	**Elizabeth Bernice Roach**

Aunts and Uncles:	Osbey
	George
	Dick
	Josie
	Betty Lee
	Ida
	Abner
		Myrtle (child: Ann Chambers)
		Leona ("Loney") :(m. a Lam) 3 children
		Nellie Marie (m. Virgil Lam)
		  children: **Gerald Allen** ("Storyteller"), **Alice**
		  ("Ridgerunner"), Hallie, Sandy, Ginger, Layton
		Icie Marie (m. C. Panopolis)
		Bess (m. Jerry Shifflett)
		  children: Addie, Sam, Elizabeth, Jerry, Virginia,
		  Bessie, John, Zena, Josh
		Mike (m. Lina Taylor)
		  children: Marie, John, Betty, Ruth, Frances,
		  Elizabeth

	[*Stepfather:* Benny Deane]	

Sibling:	**William B. Stoneberger, Jr.**
	(married Violet ?)
	  children: William B. III
	                  John
	                  Gail
	                  Eric
		Half-Siblings:
		Lucy Deane (m. Fred Fewell and, later, Floyd Morris)
		  child: Floyd "Buddy" Morris
		Helen Marie Deane (m. Jimmy Graham)
		  children: Kelly, Mike
		Kenneth Deane (never married)

JOHN W. STONEBERGER

Married Helen ("Hallie") Louise Breeden Rife

Children: Ruth Ann Stoneberger (married Stuart W. Nesbitt)
                children*:
                    Stuart W. Jr. (m. Julia McCaffery;
                        children**: Stuart W. III, Aubrey J.)
                    Eric Wayne
                    Mary Allison
                    Francine Margaret (m. Matthew K. Clark
                      children**: Andrew K., Rachel Bernice)
                    Regina Marie
                    Madeline Elizabeth
                    Bonita "Bonnie" Louise
            Betty Lou Stoneberger (married Richard Almarode)
              child*: Betty Jane
            (married Vernon J. Wargo)
              child*: Vernon J. ("Jamie")
            (married Dean Weers)

Married Virginia Collier Sealock   *Stepchildren:* Charles Sealock
                                                          child*: Annette
                                           Charlotte Sealock Marcus
                                                 children*: Rodney, Bradley

---

* John Stoneberger's grandchildren
** John Stoneberger's great-grandchildren

PATC Historical Books on the Blue Ridge Mountains

The Blue Hills of Maryland: History Along the Appalachian Trail on South Mountain and the Catoctins, by Paula M. Strain (1993). The author, a PATC volunteer trail overseer on South Mountain, conducted extensive research for this detailed history of the lands, legends, and people along the AT in western Maryland. Here you will learn of the small towns; the Antietam, Catoctin, and upper Monocacy valleys; and the railroads, canal, trolley, and trails that served the people who lived there. 315pp. illus. (#PC-310. $14.00/$11.20)

Shenandoah Secrets: The Story of the Park's Hidden Past, by Carolyn and Jack Reeder (1991). The authors have uncovered many secrets hidden in the Shenandoah National Park's forest and underneath its briary tangles. The book is divided into three major sections: "Through the Gap" covers the park from east to west through Thornton, Swift Run, and Rockfish Gaps; "Along the Drive" and "Beside the Trails" describe points of interest north to south, from Skyline Drive to Black Rock Springs. 184pp. 125 photographs. (#PC-270 $12.95/$10.35)

Shenandoah Heritage: The Story of the People Before the Park, by Carolyn and Jack Reeder (1988). Preserves the substance and flavor of the way of life of the people who lived in the mountains of the Park many years ago. 87pp. illus. (#PC-250 $6.00/$4.80)

Shenandoah Vestiges: What the Mountain People Left Behind, by Carolyn and Jack Reeder (1980). Pictures and prose about farm sites, graves, and artifacts left by the former inhabitants of the Shenandoah National Park. 71pp. illus. (#PC-260 $5.00/$4.00)

The Dean Mountain Story, by Gloria Dean (1982). The story of how James and Sarah Dean and their children left the valley and lived out their lives on Dean Mountain, now a part of the Shenandoah National Park. 80pp. (#PC-240 $5.50/$4.40)

Lost Trails and Forgotten People: The Story of Jones Mountain, by Tom Floyd (1985). The author talks about the mountain and the people who lived there before the formation of the Shenandoah National Park. Part of the great drama of human events, this story of Jones Mountain begins with the Indian settlements of about 10,000 BC, the first Europeans in the 1720s, and continues through the many human uses of the land and its final incorporation into a national parkland. 160pp. (#PC-230 $7.50/$6.00)

Breaking Trail in the Central Appalachians, by David Bates. 1987. The history of the PATC from its formation in 1927 through 1942. 194pp. (#PC-210 $12.50/$10.00)

The PATC publishes many other books of interest to hikers and backpackers, including detailed maps and trail guides for the AT and other trails in northern and western Virginia, Maryland, southern Pennsylvania, West Virginia, and the District of Columbia. For more information, contact the PATC at 118 Park Street, S.E., Vienna, Virginia 22180 or call (703) 242-0315.

The Potomac Appalachian Trail Club was founded in 1927 by seven hiking enthusiasts whose dream was a 2,000-mile trail from Maine to Georgia. In the following years, they and others completed the longest footpath in the world, the Appalachian Trail. The task of the Club's 4,000 members today is to keep that dream alive by maintaining a 240-mile section of the Appalachian Trail (from Pine Grove Furnace in Pennsylvania to Rockfish Gap in Virginia). Thirty-one similar volunteer trail clubs are responsible for the balance of the AT. The PATC also maintains more than 500 miles of additional trails, including the 144-mile Big Blue Trail.